SAVOR

Interactive Intimacy with the King of Kings

VAL SCHNACKENBERG

Savor

ISBN 979-8-9859232-6-1- *paperback*
  979-8-9859232-7-8- *ebook*

To Alex, Ari, Broxton, Shaker, and Hollis—grandkids who bring
the best kind of pride to me and tons of laughter. You show
me the heavenly Father's creativity and playfulness!

To Nate, Liz, Andy, and Ashley—stellar humans who love
Jesus; friends as well as sons and daughters-in-love.

To Bob—my travel partner, voice of wisdom and reason; your stability,
loyalty, love, and close walk with Christ have been a rock to me.

Above all, *Savor* is dedicated to Jesus—my Savior, my
King, my love. This book is all about and for you.

CONTENTS

Introduction   9

Chapter 1.   Who Is This King? (Part 1)   21

Chapter 2.   Who Is This King? (Part 2)   27

Chapter 3.   Invitations   33

Chapter 4.   The Witnesses   37

Chapter 5.   The Foundation of Intimacy   41

Chapter 6.   Self-image: Spirit or Fallen?   47

Chapter 7.   Guilt   52

Chapter 8.   Rest   55

Chapter 9.   A House of Wine   59

Chapter 10.   Centering Prayer and the Silence of God   63

Chapter 11.   The Real Journey   68

Chapter 12.   Dark Night of the Soul   75

Chapter 13.   One Step Ahead   81

Chapter 14.   Marriage   84

Chapter 15.   Mutual Praise   89

Chapter 16.   Invitation to Trust   92

Chapter 17.   Winds of Adversity   95

Chapter 18.   Second Dark Night   100

Chapter 19.   The Fight   108

Chapter 20.   The Face of God   114

Chapter 21.   The Finding   119

Chapter 22.   Supernatural Beginnings   124

Chapter 23.   Reflect and Review   128

Chapter 24.   Invitations Going Forward   133

Acknowledgments   141

Appendix   143

Notes   145

savor (sa-ver)

Verb

1. To enjoy slowly; to chew food or relish an experience slowly, in order to appreciate it as much as possible.[1]

2. To appreciate fully; enjoy or relish.[2]

INTRODUCTION

"Jesus loves me, this I know—for the Bible tells me so."

I listened as my friend continued: "But . . . how can I be certain? Through thick and thin? I want to be able to know with certainty that his love is real. I'm praying, but he's pretty silent."

I've heard this statement or variations of it repeatedly in recent months. Scripture's words assure us of God's love, but puzzling twists and turns occur in our relationship with him. Heartache or grief suddenly burst upon us, and we question if God really cares. Prayers go unanswered, sometimes for years. The Spirit seems to withdraw at times, and we may wonder if Jesus is real at all.

Savor is a guide for a journey, a journey into the love of God. Song of Solomon offers insight as we observe the king's actions and the response of the Shulamite. Reading from the viewpoint that we are the Shulamite and Jesus is the king, we enter more deeply into our own story—a story with highs and lows. Intimacy expands as we watch the tender, exuberant, masterful actions of the king and allow the Holy Spirit to pour this person's love into our souls.

Intimacy Is Conditional

Intimacy is defined as *an ever more close, familiar, affectionate and loving relationship* with another.[3] Jesus's affection, his closeness, and his "personality" become deeper and sharper as we grow in our experience of him. Although the bedrock of God's love for us is unconditional—we do nothing to either earn or sustain it—intimacy with him is conditional. Intimacy requires a response to love. Taking an "I'll just wait and see" attitude makes us like the guy in Matthew 25:28 who buried his talent. The parable of the sower reveals four types of soil in our hearts: the soils of hardness, shallowness, distractedness, and good soil, which is ready for love and intimacy. At any given time any or all of these soil types may be present in a single heart, but intimacy involves moving toward healthy soil. What is the condition of my heart's soil? Of yours?

Mutual Trust

During a process of deepening intimacy, it is not only us who grow to trust; Jesus himself must know he can trust us. "For the eyes of the Lord run to and fro throughout the whole earth, to give strong support to those whose heart is blameless toward him" (2 Chronicles 1:9).

God is peering out across the planet, looking for hearts of worship: humans who thirst, who are quick to invite his search of their lives, and who are willing to turn from the world's sparkles in order to be close to him. These attributes make up a "blameless" person (Psalm 19:13). To these hearts God opens more and more of himself and his truth, and intimacy deepens supernaturally. While on earth Jesus had flocks of followers: the seventy, the twelve, and the three. He also loved Mary, Martha, Lazarus, and perhaps others as friends. These concentric circles of intimacy and trust in each relationship feed him uniquely.

A Tennis Match

I like to think of a relationship with Jesus as a sort of slow tennis game: he "serves" me a thought from Scripture or an experience of himself. I reflect. I notice my reaction to his tennis ball and then volley it back—asking questions, letting him know how I feel about his response (verbally or in writing). I listen with awareness of the still, small voice within. He returns the ball with his response to my response, and so forth.

Rather than receiving some cool thought from Jesus and simply journaling or filing it away, we smack the tennis ball back to him, noticing our response both emotionally, cognitively, and in our bodies. Naming emotions with the use of a feelings wheel[4] is helpful. (A tip when using this wheel: **In general**, the words on the top half of the wheel are often fruits of the flesh or the result of fiery darts from the enemy. The bottom half can be fruits of the Spirit. When my feelings are orbiting around the top half, I find it helpful to look at the opposite "pie slice" in the bottom half, asking the Holy Spirit what opposite words or feelings he might want to birth within me.)

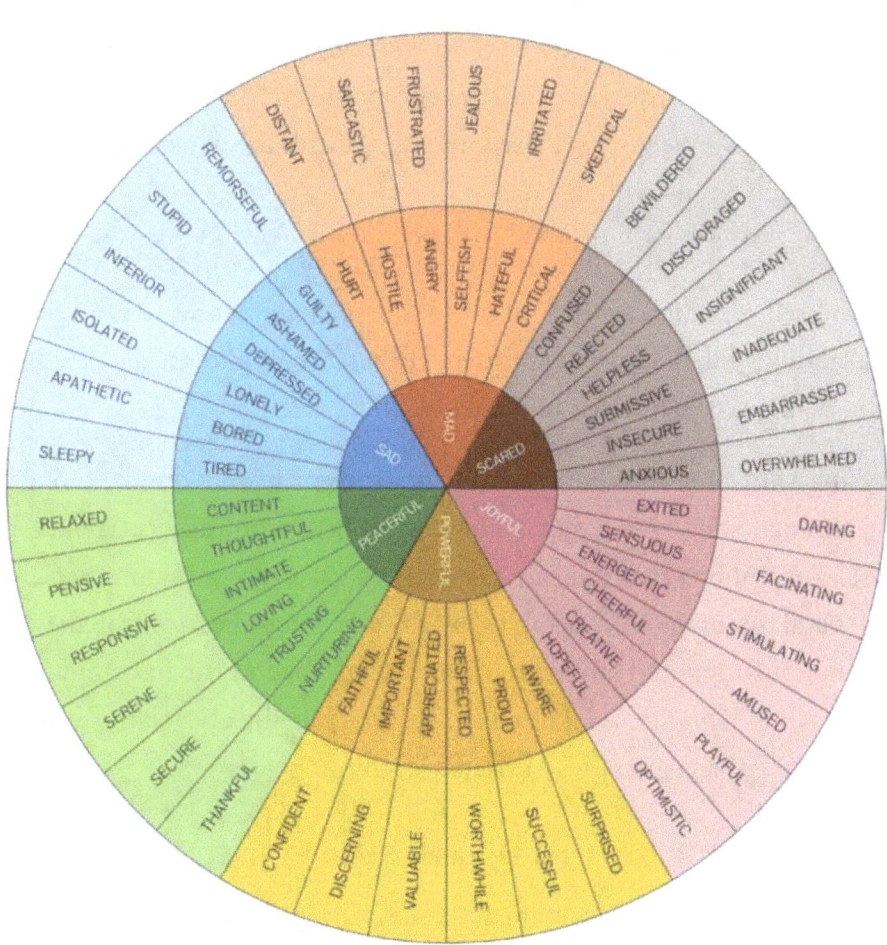

You may have heard the expression "*Name it to tame it.*" Naming an exact emotion can help us make sense of and begin to process what we're feeling. This wheel not only helps name what we're experiencing inside—it also brings cohesion between our feelings and thoughts as we give words to feelings and as we tell the Lord precisely how we feel. (He already knows how we feel, of course; verbalizing it to him simply broadens communication, strengthens trust, and increases the sense that he "gets" us.) Noticing our body's reactions of clenching or tightness also helps us know what is going on inside. As we monitor our inner reactions and share these responses with the Lord, intimacy naturally deepens. This intimacy helps us become aware of how he seems in his response back to us (patient? empathetic? with a shimmer of a chuckle?). Most of us are already skilled in relationship-building with other humans as we learn to share with increasing vulnerability and truth. We listen and ask questions when appropriate and "read" the other person's reactions or moods. We just do these same things with the person of Christ, and I call this "playing tennis" with him.

This tennis game process presupposes our being able to hear the voice of the Spirit. God self-identifies as the "Word" in John chapter 1; a word is a vehicle for communication, either spoken or written. He has a voice and speaks all languages of Earth. As the Word, he loves to communicate!

Conversing with him isn't limited to words spoken in our minds, though; we tune in through song lyrics, movie lines, and words from others. We are aware of physical sensations that indicate his nearness. We gaze at nature, sensing his attributes and listening to the parables he whispers to our hearts through what we see. For months I ignored an inner sense that I needed music to commune with him. I thought, "*Yeah, yeah, I'll listen . . . maybe.*" I finally obeyed the nudge, and music has become a primary way I relate with him.

How Does He Seem?

In human relationships of deepening intimacy, both parties must feel emotionally safe with each other; that need is the exact same with God. It takes time and faith to believe John 10, not just intellectually (that I as his sheep know his voice) but also in knowing and experiencing his voice when it is loud or silent. Part of deepening intimacy is to assert that the Spirit's job is to lead me into all truth (John 16:13) and to enjoy with delight the Spirit expanding my experience of that truth. This isn't just some ethereal, spiritual occurrence; Jesus presents his companionship to our earthly, messy human needs and situations. We bring to him the stuff of everyday life—along with how we're reacting to that life—and we find him right there. We embrace what is and find Jesus there.

How does Jesus seem to me right now? and *How am I responding to him?* are questions important to growing in intimacy. Another way to express this idea might be *What's his vibe?* If that seems a bit too casual, *What emotion or reaction is he expressing now?* We may assume that our God is always steady, with little or no emotion most of the time, but Scripture presents him as a *feeling* God. Consider his emotion in Exodus 32:10: "Let me alone, that my wrath may burn hot against them [Israel] and I may consume them." God's emotion here is strong and frightening!

Or think of Jesus in John 11:33–35, weeping at the tomb of Lazarus. Knowing that he planned to turn Mary's weeping into joy not ten minutes into the future by raising Lazarus from the dead, he nevertheless expresses strong empathy for and to her, entering into her grief and *feeling* it by joining her in her tears.

Or tap into Jesus's joy in Luke 10 after the seventy-two returned from their ministry journey, where it's recorded that he was *rejoicing in the Spirit* (verse 21). He feels things, just as we do. A tennis-match-type of relationship means we learn to become increasingly aware of how he's responding and revealing himself with all the emotions that he encompasses. Does he show delight? Is he yearning? Majestic and commanding? You'll find space to note your observations in this journal *(Selah* sections*);* take your time to process your thoughts. In whatever way he manifests himself in any given moment, he is always peace; he is safe and never in a hurry.

The Characters

As mentioned, the king in Song of Solomon is Jesus. The Shulamite is you. You will be encouraged to feel the embrace of the king both imaginatively and emotionally, to sense what it's like to be held, pursued, told honoring words, and gazed at with love and desire. Does this sound uncomfortable? Some of us will be nervous—does my understanding of God include him caressing me? Kissing me? Try to sift out culture's erotic imagery and sexually charged focus and instead take in the words of Jesus (paraphrased from Matthew 7:11): "If you, then, being evil, know how to kiss and hug your child and family members, how to lavish praise and encouragement along with needed direction, how much more will your father in heaven."

Trust the indwelling Spirit to lead you into God's unique affection for you: "But as his anointing teaches you about everything, and is true, and is no lie—just as it has taught you, abide in him" (1 John 2:27).

The Metaphors

Gardens and vineyards play prominent roles in the Song of Solomon (also referred to as "Song of Songs" throughout this book). For our purposes, the gardens and vineyards represent basically the same thing: our inner experience with the Lord, that place we mean when we lay a hand on our chests and say, "He's in here." Our garden is our private, inner relationship with God. Other metaphors appear (foxes, walls, veils), and they will be introduced with their meanings in later chapters.

A Right-Brain Book

The Song of Solomon was written as poetry, a song/tableau originally, placing it more in the realm of "right-brain" (creative, emotional) art than as a "left-brain" (cognitive) study. We're taught that to really know God's love will *surpass* our knowledge (Ephesians 3:19) and that to know his peace will *surpass* understanding (Philippians 4:7). To facilitate this *cognition-surpassing* interaction with the king in the chapters of this poetic book, we will employ various right-brain modalities such as *lexio divina, visio divina, and* Immanuel journaling.

Lexio divina (lectio divina—divine reading) is a traditional contemplative practice of scriptural reading, meditation, and prayer intended to promote communion with God and to increase understanding of God's Word.[5]

Visio divina (divine seeing) is similar to *lexio divina* in that it invites the viewer to commune with the Spirit of God but by encountering him or characteristics about him through images rather than the written word of Scripture.[6] These images can come from art, photographs, scenes in nature, or from life in general. They can be thought of as visual parables that express truth, such as those Jesus taught.

Immanuel journaling is a fresh way to journal, a writing exercise that helps us to explore our life events (especially our interior lives, including our thoughts, feelings, and body sensations) with our good God, Immanuel. It is a simple process to help us become aware of God's compassionate presence in the painful as well as mundane moments of our lives.[7]

These contemplative exercises will be presented in the following pages. Additionally, I have a public playlist on Spotify called "Savor, the Book" with a song corresponding to each chapter. To find the playlist, open the Spotify app and search "Savor, the book" by Val Schnackenberg. Then, once in the playlist, you can listen to each song when directed to in the *Selah* reflections at the end of each chapter. To see the lyrics, tap on the "Now Playing View" on a song. Then swipe up from the bottom of the screen, and you will see the song's lyrics that scroll in real time as the song plays. Additionally, you can find the playlist in the appendix on page 143 and listen to the songs on your own music streaming service or search them in YouTube. Listening to these songs and reading any unfamiliar lyrics will aid your brain in assimilating the message from each chapter.

Selah

Throughout this study you will also notice liberal use of the word *selah*—a directive word from the Psalms that means *pause*.

Pause when you see this word. I mean it. *Stop*.

(That means don't just keep reading!)

Savor.

Taste and see his goodness.

Use your senses. Imagine, notice, feel, see, *savor* how the ideas affect you.

No relationship will survive long, let alone deepen in intimacy, if one partner offers a quick listen or mumbles a few words and then walks away. Building intimacy takes time. It also takes disciplining our "monkey brain" and pinball feelings; the prayer exercises in this guide are designed to do just that when practiced with dedication and care. Intimacy invites us to linger, waiting on the words of our lover.

Take Some Deep Breaths

In *Selah* pauses you'll be invited to breathe deeply. Why deep breathing? Research shows that it affects our brain activity by stimulating the vagus nerve, which regulates the "fight or flight" reflex. This nerve activates neurotransmitters that tell our nervous system to relax, to calm down. Deep breathing also brings oxygen into our system, which lowers our heartbeat and stabilizes our blood pressure.

Neuroplasticity is the brain's capacity to continue growing and evolving in response to life experiences, to create new neurons and build new networks, and to change patterns of thought and reactions over time.[8] Deep breathing and a practice called "centering prayer" (explained and presented for practice in chapter 10) are a powerful one-two punch that will over time and with practice lower anxiety, quiet fear, and greatly enhance intimacy with the Spirit.

Taking time to pause *(Selah)* reorients your brain to Christ and his intimate messages of love and encouragement. Deep breathing settles your mind and spirit to welcome Jesus's ministry of making himself more experientially real. This is perhaps the point of this entire guide—slow down to receive his timeless ministry. Live a *Selah* life!

Love as an Unscripted Dance

The Song of Songs reveals a person, the king, who loves perfectly. It also provides a pathway for his love interest—us—to enter an ever-deepening reciprocal relationship with our king. Intimacy with Christ under the guidance of the Song of Solomon presents imaginatively like a dance—non-scripted, following desire rather than duty.

Dancing doesn't come naturally to most of us; we need to learn how. We stumble over our feet at first as we try to follow steps from the instructor. We practice, over and over. Gradually the movements become more fluid. Imperceptibly, our cognition takes a back seat and we relax into our partner (Jesus). We allow him to lead, and our body subconsciously moves with him. A good lead dance partner anticipates the next moves and, with whispers of subtle pressure, ushers our feet and body into position. This "dance" with the Lord corresponds figuratively to the "rest" in Hebrews 4, a life lived in the sabbath rest of God. He leads. We follow, almost subconsciously. And we dance.

Love for Its Own Sake

The Song of Solomon reveals a love between us and Christ that is enjoyed for its own sake, far from something I must learn in order to _____ (fill in the blank—*have a better ministry, be a better spouse or parent,* or *master another thing in order to perform and make God love me better).* We can be quick to make everything a task with some objective to be met! But the Song presents our relationship with God as something very different from a cause-and-effect, basically cerebral method of approaching him. The relationship of intimacy presented is described as a long, refreshing vacation of exploring Another, wandering at whim where the relationship takes us. It shows the relationship simply as something to be enjoyed for its own sake. There are no rules to follow—just a beckoning invitation to explore divine love that magically opens as we go.

Go at Your Own Pace

You're invited to take each short chapter and spend as many days in each as you'd like, to *relish* the experience as the definition of *savor* so aptly expresses. Go at the pace Jesus sets for you. Dig more deeply with your insights; ask for more from him. Sharing the experience with several others in a small group would be most helpful as you see a compounded picture of Jesus emerge through others' experiences of him.

Selah

Take some deep breaths. Remember—this calms your nervous system, brings in fresh oxygen, and enables a quieter mind so as to hear the King of Kings. Rest quietly for two to ten minutes, reviewing and savoring the parts of this introduction that spoke to you.

When you feel ready, look at the pictures below (this is called *visio divina*). As you gaze, reflect on the questions.

Which picture[9] above captures the essence of your inner life or your relationship with the Lord most of the time?

What stands out from each picture; what do you notice?

_____

_____

_____

What emotions or body sensations do you feel as you look at each one?

_____

_____

_____

Talk with the Lord about your answer. Listen for any whispers or encouragement from him as you share with him. Note anything you want to remember.

_____

_____

_____

What would you like your inner garden—your place of communion and abiding with Christ—to *look* like if it were pictured as a painting?

_____

_____

_____

What would you like the *atmosphere* of your inner garden to feel like? You can refer to the feelings wheel on page 11 to prime the pump of vocabulary if that seems helpful.

_____

_____

_____

1

WHO IS THIS KING?
(PART 1)

To be honest, the Song of Solomon has seemed out of place with the rest of Scripture. It seems too erotic and body-part-centric for my understanding of the Bible in general and of God in particular. *Why did God include this book in the canon of Scripture?* I've wondered. After months of study, poring over various translations and commentaries, I've come to believe that this book reveals parts of God's makeup, his "personality," if you will, that don't come out as sharply in other books—parts such as he is a lover. He's passionate. His emotional desire is intense toward his people. The Song of Songs reveals his love for and excitement about relationships in general and acts out the biblical husband/wife metaphor of Christ and his bride.

So before opening the first chapter of Song of Solomon, it's good to lay a brief scriptural foundation about love, relationships, and the king who is the star of the book: Jesus.

Love. From the Beginning . . . to the End

Consider the primacy of love and weddings throughout Scripture:

- Genesis begins with God's creation of a garden. The word *Eden* in Hebrew means "pleasure"—a perfect nest for a man and a woman to enjoy pleasure with each other as well as with God himself.

- The canon of Scripture ends with Jesus's marriage supper drawing near (a party! love being celebrated!)

- Hosea presents abiding love in the context of cheating.

- Isaiah 54:5 states, "Your Maker is your husband."

- Jesus is called "beloved" by God.

- A summary from 1 John: "God *is* love."

- The word usually used for *love* in Song of Songs is the same word that describes the affection Jonathan felt for David, so it's not just a feminine, emotional concept.

- "Love" is mentioned in Scripture anywhere from 551 to 714 times, depending on which words are searched in the original languages.

Uncorrupted love is front and center in God's mind for his creation, for his identity is love itself. We are made in his image, so we are made for and have the capacity to give love. God wants emotional, spiritual, and pleasurable intimacy with us that bears benefit to our physical bodies and psychological makeup as we learn to relax and trust him. What does Scripture teach about this Person whose very makeup is love?

He Wants and Needs Us

I've heard it said that God is the self-existent one, needing nothing. While this is in one sense possibly true, consider how he began this planet in the first place.

God made a garden of pleasure (*Eden* means pleasure.) It was a beautiful, sinless, climate-perfect, sublime place. Then he fashioned a man and a woman to live there. And he wanted to share this place of pleasure with them. He walked with them in the cool of the day. . . . What did they do in there? I imagine they reveled in love and delight. It's not recorded how they related, but this before-the-fall scene is fodder for our sanctified imaginations to bloom under the sunlight of his love and desire for us.

King Jesus needs us. Think about another garden, the Garden of Gethsemane. In Matthew 26 Jesus asked Peter, James, and John to watch and pray with him. They kept falling asleep in spite of his repeated exhortation to stay awake. Do we consider how much he needed them? His words indicate desperation as he implored them to stay awake. These aren't the words of a man who is self-sufficient. Can we know him in his need of us?

He Has Great Emotion

God's name *Yahweh* has been translated into English from the Hebrew as "I Am Who I Am" or "The Existing One." Hebrew scholars also translate this as "He Who Causes to Be." But according to Shelomo Dov Goitein, a Jewish and Arabic studies scholar, God proclaimed this name for himself to Moses at Mt. Horeb in Exodus 3 while he was living in Midian. Midian corresponds to present-day Arabia. Because "YHWH" has no vowels, the Hebrew and Arabic transliteration of this word yields different meanings. The Arabic transliteration of YHWH means "The Impassioned One."[10] Translating Exodus 3:14 in this manner, we see God announcing himself to Moses: "I Am Impassioned."

Impassioned: "to be filled with or demonstrating intense emotion"[11]

This proto-Arabic meaning of YHWH yields depth to God's words in Exodus 34:14: "You shall worship no other god, for YHWH, whose name is [Impassioned], is a jealous God."

Jesus as our God is filled with great emotion toward us and shows it by jealousy when we turn from him. Think about this. Do we ever consider how our messing around with idols or our stiff-arming him affects him emotionally? Consider his response to Israel in Hosea (they were cheating with other gods): "How can I give you up, O Ephraim? . . . My heart recoils within me; my compassion grows warm and tender" (Hosea 11:8). Think about the heart of God recoiling within him when his people give themselves to idols. I wonder how he brings himself back to warmth and tenderness after we invoke his jealousy through bad choices.

For myself, this journey into the emotional love of Jesus has come slowly. In my childhood my parents said they loved me and my sister (and for sure, they did), but I recall lots (and lots) of spankings and admonitions that "children should be seen and not heard." Later in my life when a retreat speaker taught on how we all want love, I remember a swift knee-jerk reaction inside me: "*No,* I don't want love! I want **safety**." Love seemed hurtful, cutting. Love left a lot of confusion and uncertainty. I wanted nothing to do with it for years.

I remember the day as I walked in the forest near our Colorado home when Jesus invaded my Spotify playlist. The current song I was listening to ended, and the song "Who Am I?" by Casting Crowns began. Whether this was a supernatural song switch or simply my phone shifting in my pocket, I have no idea. But immediately in my mind's eye the Lord began slow dancing with me, right there on the path. The forest scene around me seemed to shape-shift ever so slightly as I felt the sensation of being in his strong arms. I could also "see" the two of us from above. As we danced, Jesus had a look of tenderness and love on his face that took my breath away. I hadn't asked for this experience, hadn't even considered this could be a thing. My arms went up around his torso as we swayed to this song of worship and love. Heart thumping wildly, emotions—peace, joy, ecstatic-ness—took over my brain. Thankfully the trail was empty that day; I would have been a weird sight to any fellow hikers! Processing it later, I definitely wanted more (*That was love? Yes—please!*).

Paul also had some apparently deeply moving times with the Lord. Second Corinthians 5:13 states, "If we are beside ourselves, it is for God." According to the text note in The Passion Translation of this verse, the Greek word for "beside ourselves," *existemi,* means to be "outside of oneself in a state of blissful ecstasy and filled with pleasure" and "to come into another state of consciousness of being lost in wonder and amazement." Paul apparently experienced being in this place of unimaginable ecstasy and stated that this was **for God.** Might this type of experience be what he was referring to in 2 Corinthians 12:4 when he "heard things that cannot be told, which man may not utter"?

Imagine for a minute being constantly pursued by gentle, powerful, emotional warmth: a continual assurance of non-condemning welcome, enjoyment, and delight coming from Jesus inside. This living, breathing presence laughs, roars with joy, looks with dizzying depth into our eyes, gently kisses us with longing that's at once holy, tender, and passionate. Things engendered by the world—comparison, stress, fear, anxiety—shift to the side of our focus and then slide off into oblivion as the person of our king wraps his arms around our spirit. *This* is the message and promise of the Song of Solomon. And this love is the longing of every human heart.

Selah

Get into a comfortable position and begin to relax your mind and body by taking some deep breaths. Recall the benefits of pausing and breathing deeply mentioned in the introduction. Take at least sixty seconds for this, turning your awareness (repeatedly if necessary) to the peace and presence of the Lord.

Listen to song #1 in the Spotify public playlist "*Savor, the Book*" as you rest in the Lord. (This playlist is also included in the appendix for those who don't have Spotify. You can search the songs on YouTube or in other music streaming sites.)

When you sense an inner quietness, reflect on these questions:

What do you honestly *think* about your God having strong emotion?

_____

_____

Now allow your cognition to quiet as you consider your *feelings* about Christ having strong emotion toward and about you. How do you experience this? Return to the feelings wheel on (page 11) and jot down the words that capture your reaction.

_____

_____

What might be reasons for the words you chose? Talk with the Lord about this.

_____

_____

Prayerfully ask the Holy Spirit to highlight words from the bottom half of the feelings wheel that he wants you to revel in as he wraps you in his love. Take your time with this. What words stand out?

_____

_____

How do you respond to him now as he expresses his love for you in the words you wrote down?

_____

_____

_____

_____

2

WHO IS THIS KING?
(PART 2)

W**E CONTINUE OUR STROLL THROUGH** S**CRIPTURE, CONSIDERING HOW IT PORTRAYS THE** K**ING OF** K**INGS.**

He Is Intensely Personal and Wants to Know and Enjoy *Me*

Song of Solomon 2:2 records King Jesus telling the Shulamite, "As a lily among [thorns], so is my love among the young women." In this verse he gives the Shulamite the gift of preferring her above others. We might say he's telling her she is his favorite. But God has no favorites, right?

In one sense, yes. It's been said, "God has no favorites, but he has intimates." However, in another sense his love is so vast, so without boundaries that I believe he can look each of us in the eye and say, "You're my favorite," and not be lying.

In his book *Imagine Heaven* author John Burke records stories of people who have died, been certified as dead, and are then revived and brought back to life. They relate what happened to them in the interim. Some see and enter heaven; some do not. Most see Jesus, even those who are of other faiths. Many of the accounts are from university professors, surgeons, and other high-profile people who have a lot to lose and nothing to gain by fabricating details.

The account of a man named Dean supports how personal the Lord's love is for each of his people:

> God the Father (was) singing back to each and every being giving him praise. He was singing an individual love song to each of his creations. The song was alive and seemed to go inside of the beings it was meant for....That is what was going on in Heaven. Father God was expressing his love for each being and they were expressing their love for him.[12]

Dean goes on to say,

> Jesus is more beautiful, wonderful and glorious than I can explain . . . everything about Jesus is love. His love for you is so personal it seems as if it is only for you. His love is alive. It is more than just a sense . . . it was like I was the only one he loved in all of his creation. I knew he loved others, but it seemed as if I was the only one.[13]

I'm his favorite. You're his favorite!

Humans' Actions Affect Him

Recall the account of Noah and his ark from Genesis 6–8. Noah was a "righteous man, blameless in his generation. Noah walked with God" (Genesis 6:9). After building the ark and living in it for over a year, he came out onto dry ground and immediately sacrificed to God. "And when the Lord smelled the pleasing aroma, he said in his heart, 'I will never again curse the ground because of man'" (8:21). God has kept this promise for ages, and all because a human voluntarily did something for, toward, and in obedience to Him. Noah's action affected God, making him take a vow that continues to this day.

Notice that God didn't just *see* Noah sacrificing; he *smelled the soothing aroma*. Noah's decision to sacrifice brought God to a place of being "soothed, quieted, and tranquil," according to the Hebrew. He is a sensual God, and our actions affect his emotional state.

Sempor Maior

We follow a God who is *sempor maior*—someone who is always greater than us. His thoughts and ways—always higher. There is always more of him to know and experience.

We can be like a horse tethered to the peg of our own understanding of what God is like, able to consume the treasure of who he is only within the range of our history and experience. He calls us out of our cognitive minds into the free range of sensual (that just means to use our senses) and emotional exploration with him—nothing is off limits. The tether is removed, and we roam free and easy into the hugeness and wildness of the love of Christ.

My analytical mind was attempting to understand why the Lord was becoming increasingly physically affectionate in my mind's eye. He was constantly hugging me. I reasoned to Jesus, "You're doing this because you see that I was raised in a very strict environment—that to little Val, touch often involved spanks. And you're trying to show me how your love is comfortable, that being embraced can actually be safe. Is that it?"

Jesus was quiet a moment. Then he said carefully, "I'm glad you're understanding that love and touch can be a good thing. But actually I just really like hugging you!" Broad smile.

He has a Body, Now . . . Flesh and Bone in a Heavenly Sense

This might be obvious, but as we experience the embrace of Jesus in the coming weeks, we need to understand that this idea of his having arms, legs, a torso, and a head isn't some ethereal, figurative thing.

Think about how you'd react if you were present in Luke 24:36–43 when the two Emmaus road men were recounting their encounter with the post-dead Jesus:

> While they were still discussing all of this, Jesus suddenly appeared right in front of their eyes! Startled and terrified, the disciples were convinced they were seeing a ghost. Standing there among them he said, "Be at peace. I am the living God. Don't be afraid. Why are you so frightened? Don't let doubt enter your hearts. See my pierced hands and feet. See

for yourselves, it is I, standing here alive. Touch me and know that my wounds are real. A spirit does not have a body of flesh and bone as you see that I have." Then he showed them his pierced hands and feet and let them touch his wounds. The disciples were ecstatic, yet dumbfounded, unable to fully comprehend it. Knowing that they were still wondering if he was real, Jesus said, "Here, let me show you. Give me something to eat." They handed him a piece of broiled fish and some honeycomb. And they watched him eat.

Jesus was certifiably dead. And now he's standing among them, inviting them to touch him and feel his physical presence. Although this was prior to his ascension, Paul assures us in Philippians 3:21 that he still has a body—a glorified body. But what difference does this make for us in our quest for deeper intimacy?

Selah

Pause. Slow your breathing and your cognitive mind for a moment. Breathe deeply and allow your body to relax. With each deep exhale, release any bodily tension you feel, allowing yourself to sag into the chair or floor that is supporting you. Take time with this.

When you're ready, begin to imagine the scene in Luke 24. Read the passage above again. You are one of the disciples who are present. Jesus has recently died, although some are now saying they've seen him. How are you feeling initially, with Jesus having died?

Describe the scene above as you see it in your mind's eye. Colors? Smells? Record your observations:

_____

_____

Suddenly Jesus is right here in front of you—definitely *not* dead. He looks you in the eyes and says, "[your name], come here and touch me." How do you react? Close your eyes and enter into this scene. Feel your feelings as if you are there with him.

_____

_____

Now accept his invitation and touch him: hand, shoulder, head, whatever part of him you want to touch. How does his body feel to you? What message does your heart receive from feeling his body and from seeing his eyes look into yours?

_____

_____

Continuing the scene, he asks for something to eat. You get it for him. He eats it, still watching your eyes as he chews. What do his eyes convey to you? Is there an invitation from him?

_____

_____

How does this imaginative reading of Scripture affect your sense of and desire for intimacy with him? Tell him in detail. Listen for his response to your sharing; be aware of how he seems to you. Record any feelings or thoughts:

_____

_____

_____

Now look over the sections about Christ our king in this chapter and the previous one. Which one or two of his characteristics mentioned do you sense yourself longing to experience more of?

_____

_____

Listen to song #2 in the "*Savor,* the Book" playlist. Enjoy the message of this song!

Being Practical . . .

As we begin chapter one of Solomon's Song on the next page, here are a few fundamentals to keep in mind:

- We *believe* this intense, personal, deeply satisfying love of Jesus; we don't strive to achieve it or to feel it. "Believe that you have received it [past tense], and it will be yours" (Mark 11:24) is the bedrock under our feet. We don't waffle or question the fact of his love; there is no being driven and tossed like a wave of the sea. His love is a *given.* It's solid.

- We *position ourselves to receive* his self-revelation. We *imagine* under the sanctifying tutelage of the Holy Spirit and of the Word of God and truth that we know.

- We *expect* our perceptions and experiences of him to expand.

- We *test* what we receive—always and first through the biblical truth about God. Does my experience of him line up? Does it bring peace and life—or darkness—to my soul? We also ask people whose walks with God and integrity we trust.

- We *trust* that we actually have the mind of Christ working with ours (1 Corinthians 2:16).

Ready?

The curtain of pure heavenly love is drawn back in the Song of Songs. Jesus stands in front of the curtain, inviting us to take his hand and explore with him.

3

INVITATIONS

SOLOMON'S SONG BEGINS WITH KISSES. "Let him kiss me with the kisses of his mouth! For your love is better than wine; your anointing oils are fragrant; your name is oil poured out. . . . Draw me after you; let us run. The king has brought me into his chambers" (Song of Solomon 1:2–4).

The love God has toward us is other-worldly. It is beyond our comprehension, living as we do in a darkened, fallen world. I believe Song of Solomon is replete with kisses because experiencing a kiss, when one is in love, represents the closest thing in our human experience and in our brain chemistry to the passion Jesus feels for us and wants us to feel for him.

The Passion Translation has an informative note on the above verses concerning kisses:

> There is a wordplay in the Hebrew, similar to a pun. The word for "kisses" and the word for "take a drink (wine)" is nearly the same. The implication, as seen by ancient expositors, is that God's lovers will be drunk with love, the intoxicating kisses of his mouth. The Hebrew word for "kiss" is *nashaq*, which can also mean "to equip" or "to arm (for battle)." We need his kisses to become equipped warriors for him.

Love in the Song of Songs is no sip of a fruity mocktail. Love is training for the most important role we'll ever play: at his side for eternity, ruling and reigning with him (Revelation 5:9–10).

Initial Directions

Direction for the journey into intimacy with Christ comes from these opening verses.

The Shulamite starts first with giving the king permission to love her ("Let him," 1:2), then has a request ("Draw me after you," 1:4), which is followed by the king's action ("brought me into his chambers," 1:4).

We launch into deeper intimacy with the Lord by first *giving him permission to love us* as he wants to. We yield to the action and leadership of Christ. By so doing, we declare our willingness to allow him to change our perceptions of who he is as he opens himself to us. This may not be as easy or obvious as it sounds. Consider the "kisses of his mouth" above. How do you react to a God who has a mouth that kisses passionately?

We then ask him to *draw us after himself.* "Draw me after *you*" (emphasis added). We ask to *know him*, not to simply experience warm feelings. Although healing and transformation are the fruit of this journey of intimacy, the main event is all about him and knowing/experiencing him. "Let him who boasts boast in this, that he understands and knows me" (Jeremiah 9:24). By asking to be drawn by him (this is in the passive voice), we also acknowledge that we need him to lead us; we can't draw ourselves into deeper intimacy.

He responds by *bringing us into his chambers.* This Hebrew word for *chamber* (*ḥeder*) is a "room within a room," or an inner room. This is the same word used in the Old Testament for a bedroom.

The imagery of an inner room is also reminiscent of the Most Holy Place in the temple of God:

> *A bedroom*: a place of rest, where we may most be ourselves. A place of physical love in marriage.

> *The Most Holy Place*: a realm of utmost beauty and sacredness, opened to us by the tearing of the temple curtain when Jesus died.

Putting these ideas together, we see a picture of Christ the Savior, welcoming us to relax in his home, inviting us into the joy that got him through the agonies of the cross. Deepening our intimacy with Christ happens in a place of rest, peace, love, and holiness. The sexually intimate moments that happen in a human marriage bedroom correlate to a spiritual intimacy initiated by God, within a Most Holy Place that is the king's chamber. The picture is of a high place of purity, set-apartness, sanctity, blended with rest and peace, where we are being deeply loved and kissed by God.

Selah

Stop. Breathe deeply and slowly for a few inhales/exhales. On the inhale: Take in the atmosphere that surrounds the Prince of *Peace*. Exhale: Let go of unrest inside, any stress that is trying to intrude into your inner garden with Jesus. Keep inhaling peace and exhaling stress until your mind and body calm.

Consider this chamber of Jesus—a bedroom/Most Holy Place where we meet him in intimacy. What thoughts emerge? What's your reaction to being in this place that blends rest, love, and holiness?

_____

Now consider being in this place of rest alone with Jesus. How do you feel about it? Record any words, pictures, emotions, or thoughts:

_____

_____

If you feel comfortable, verbally give him permission to love you as he wants to.

And ask him to draw you after himself.

Now listen to song #3 in the "*Savor,* the Book" playlist.

Going a bit deeper, ask the Holy Spirit to bring a picture into your mind of this chamber, this holy place of rest he's designed especially for you and him. What does it look like? Is it outside? Inside? What colors do you see? How about smells? Let this unfold in your sanctified imagination. Jot down any details you want to remember about this place.

_____

_____

_____

_____

Be aware of Jesus; how does he seem to you? As you pause and allow this place of holiness and rest to unfold, do you notice the Lord doing anything specific? What does his manner convey as he welcomes you in? Record anything you want to remember from this prayer experience.

_____

_____

_____

_____

4

THE WITNESSES

Now that we have some initial direction for proceeding, Song of Solomon 1:4 introduces "others." These shadowy characters (sometimes labeled "women of Jerusalem" or "witnesses") weren't delineated in the original text. They were added later as a response to the verbal endings and gender indications of the words. Each translation of Song of Solomon renders these differently; for our purposes, these "others" serve as heavenly encouragers, as wise mentors. Here they are cheering us on: they're delighted and joyful as we explore the love Jesus has for us and we have toward him. (Others): "We will exult and rejoice in you; we will extol your love more than wine" (1:4).

These witnesses also give caution. Three places in Song of Solomon the witnesses say, "Do not stir up or awaken love until it pleases" (2:7; 3:5; 8:4). These mentors assure us that we don't need to go faster than we feel comfortable as we explore the love of our king. Although we've yielded the leadership of this relationship to Jesus and the Holy Spirit, the pace with which we proceed is up to us, especially as he gently and powerfully reveals parts of himself we haven't known before.

We can take this process slowly and seriously as we navigate this journal. Be aware of your emotions and reactions as we progress; note them in the margins and tell them to Jesus. Whenever we sense unrest or questioning in our soul, we bring those feelings to the Lord and, when appropriate, to others whose walks with Christ we trust. It goes without saying that seeking other parts of Scripture and its wisdom is also apropos here.

Sensing the emotion and longing for relationship that Christ has toward us can be surprising and even overwhelming. It can conversely be rather *anticlimactic* if we feel a void from him. Both experiences are legitimate and rather common. The main questions "How does Jesus seem?" and "How am I reacting to his expression of himself right now?" are important to reflect on. We tell Jesus, either verbally or in writing, what we think and feel, waiting for him to answer us back. This, along with a bit of persevering faith, is all that's needed for intimacy to grow. Remember that he will be unique with each of us, consistent with Scripture but never predictable.

Selah

Deep breaths. Center your mind and awareness on the presence of Christ within and around you. Think about the delight and joy from heavenly witnesses as they see you open to his love. How do you experience this idea of heavenly beings watching you, cheering you on as you explore intimacy with Jesus?

_____

_____

_____

Now with your mind's eye, enter the chamber of rest and holiness you saw in the previous chapter. Refer back to any notes you wrote about this place of rest. Take a few moments for this; relax in your holy place of intimacy and love with the Lord. There is no condemnation or need to hurry through this.

_____

_____

_____

As you relax in this place, listen to song #4 in the "*Savor*, the Book" playlist.

Where do you see or sense Christ in this place of rest? Is he doing anything specific?

_____

_____

When you're settled, take a deep dive into your longings. What do you really want from the Lord concerning intimacy in relationship with him?

_____

_____

_____

What emotions emerge as you tap into these longings? (Refer to the feelings wheel on page 11 if it's helpful.) You may experience painful memories from people in your past or from Jesus himself regarding love. Bring any such memories and feelings to him now. Being as honest as you can, write a note to Jesus.

Jesus, right now I'm thinking . . .

_____

_____

_____

And, Jesus, right now I'm feeling . . .

_____

_____

_____

With a quiet heart and mind, ask him to write you back in response to what you wrote. This is called "Immanuel Journaling." You start by writing what you know the God of Scripture would say to you and then let the words from Scripture meld into his message to you for today.

Jesus: My beloved, I want to tell you . . .

_____

_____

_____

_____

Read over what you wrote. Using your God-given discernment, do the words from your Immanuel Journaling above sound like the Lord of Scripture? If so, agree with and receive his truth.

5

THE FOUNDATION
OF INTIMACY

JESUS: *I WANT TO TELL YOU A STORY.*

Me: *Okay! (I settle in.)*

Jesus: *Once upon a time there was a governor over a vast, beautiful kingdom of peace. The Father in heaven loved to provide all the people of this kingdom needed— food, shelter, good prosperity, good times, and good health. They lived in security and plenty; they had great joy as they shared life and possessions with each other.*

But one day a rumor came to the peoples' ears: an invading army and enemies were on their way. The governor and the people wondered what this could mean and began to imagine what might happen. Their peaceful way of life might splinter apart; food might become scarce. Anxiety set in. The governor, as he contemplated this threat to his kingdom, began to worry, and a dark cloud came upon his thinking. The people, sensing this dark cloud gathering above their land, began to store provisions, anticipating a time of lack. No one shared with others anymore, preferring to store up for themselves.

As time went on, no army actually ever came; the threat never became reality. It had been, as it turned out, a rumor. But because the governor and his kingdom still felt afraid, the dark cloud over the area became more widespread, pervading the people's thinking and feelings. The people lived out their days under the cloud, not realizing they'd been duped by a lie.

****

Jesus: *Do you understand the story?*

Me: *I think so. I'm like the governor; I'm susceptible to lies and rumors that darken my understanding of and enjoyment of all you've given me?*

Jesus: *That's right. Realize all I've bought back for you through the cross. You no longer live under clouds or rumors. I've given you an entirely new nature—new thoughts, a fresh spirit—in which to dwell. Be on your guard against the fruits of darkness stemming from your old nature that has been crucified.*

The Lord told me this story some years ago, but its message is straight out of the Song of Solomon. The Shulamite is "under" some powerful rumors:

> I am very dark, but lovely, O daughters of Jerusalem, like the tents of Kedar, like the curtains of Solomon. Do not gaze at me because I am dark, because the sun has looked upon me. My mother's sons were angry with me; they made me keeper of the vineyards, but my own vineyard I have not kept! (Song of Solomon 1:5–6)

As the Shulamite dwells in the king's bedroom/chamber of holiness, she's beginning to notice some things about herself. She realizes she's dark; she knows the sun has tanned her skin into leather, and she knows she's ugly, tainted. Her shame response kicks in ("Do not gaze at me"), and she gives the reason for this darkness: her "mother's sons" (that is, sons of her mother but from another father—this is significant) have made her work in the sun in the heat of the day. She's hot, exhausted, and unable to tend her own vineyard or care for herself.

Our Old Nature—Alive or Dead?

These "sons of another father" come from her Adamic lineage—in other words, they represent her fallen human nature, her old nature, if you will. Using the metaphor from the story above, they are the voices of rumor, fear, doubt, and lack that we all experience at some point. Their tactic is to force us to work hard, slaving in the hot sun in the heat of the day. Their objective is to drive us out of our vineyard and to prevent this place of intimacy from flourishing (*vineyard* being the metaphor in Song of Solomon for the private, holy place where we meet with Christ and deepen our intimacy with him). The fruit of living under our old nature is exhaustion; we try hard to please others and self, never seeming to achieve this, certainly never resting.

The Shulamite then says, "Tell me, you whom my soul loves, where you pasture your flock, where you make it lie down at noon; for why should I be like one who veils herself beside the flocks of your companions?" (Song of Solomon 1:7). A paraphrase of this verse: "Wait a minute! Here's this king who can't stop kissing me. He takes his flocks to a shady place of green grass and nourishment in the heat of the day! What the heck am I doing beating myself up in the sun at noon, always under a veil of shame, never getting any rest or food for myself?" Truth begins to dawn as she dwells in the king's chambers.

The Gospel—*The* Foundation for Intimacy

The gospel—Jesus dying for us to take God's punishment for our sins and removing the power of our old nature—is the only possible foundation for the freedom and enjoyment of intimacy. Without this foundation, intimacy and, in fact, a relationship with Jesus will not flourish. Why? Because our gaze will be on ourselves—how we are performing or measuring up. We never will measure up; work in the Shulamite's hot sun is never done. Intimacy demands taking a stand for Jesus: his work on the cross and his resounding "It is finished" that dealt a death blow to our old natures. Death blow as in never to resurrect again. Gone. Dead.

The problem is, just like the governor and citizens above, we listen to dark accusation and rumors; we don't police our inner critic nearly enough. So what does this foundation of the gospel mean practically for us as we navigate intimacy with Jesus?

It means to stop striving to be "good." We're already good, clothed with his righteousness. True rest springs from this fact. It means to stop fearing condemnation or accusation; there is no condemnation for us in Jesus, and there are no impending armies behind the rumors. It means to bring all the broken parts—the knee-jerk responses of our past trauma that lead us to do dumb things—to Jesus and allow him to transform **as he sees fit**. It means that there should no longer be shame about our anger, our anxiety, our sexual feelings, our drives, and our questions. It means to stop allowing others' emotions or drama to determine our behavior. It means that we no longer have to be codependent on the demands of others or on our own demands.

It means *you are enough*, and you can stop measuring your performance and worth. First John 4:17 (MSG) says, "Our standing in the world is identical with Christ's." Let this truth sink in!

John continues in the next verse: "Perfect love [expels] fear." The word *expels* in Greek is "to throw out, to cast out of doors." It's a violent word. Only the perfect and complete *love* of Jesus gets permanent (out of doors, outside where we dwell) rid of our fears, shame, and anxieties. We can't think our way out of fear or other leftovers from our old nature; rather, we sink into a love that is perfect, complete. Why live under threats, shame, and worries when we can catapult into the warm waters of perfect love?

The enemy of our intimacy with Christ—the devil—works overly hard to keep us in shame, anxiety, fear, and chained to the opinions of others. And no wonder; these "rumors" effectively bar us from the powerful delights of love and freedom Jesus has bought for us. Don't partner with the enemy. Turn instead to the most perfect, empathetic, sympathetic, masterful, wise Counselor we could ever know. He is love itself.

The Lord once showed me a picture in my mind's eye of a large room with fresh white paint and huge windows. The door had a big padlock on the inside. I asked what this represented. He answered, "This room is your mind and emotion. For too long you've allowed anything to come in here—any thought or feeling. Words of diminishment, feelings of being beaten, being worthless. It's time to have a healthy padlock; you know now what's true. You are strong in truth—so keep out what should stay out and let in only words and feelings that echo mine!" The picture of this white, bright, comfortable room with a big ol' padlock powerfully helps keep my old nature where it belongs: in a graveyard.

There's Goodness in Me!

Seeking his love and responding to it, while resting fully on the completed work of Christ, opens the door to a fresh experience of our own goodness. This goodness is achieved and bestowed by his death on the cross, and by grace alone. We're free to breathe the rarified air of heaven, free to revel in the garments of righteousness he's given us.

Selah

Settle in with Jesus while taking deep breaths. Allow your body to relax, readying your spirit to commune with him. Turn your inner gaze upon him as you breathe in fresh oxygen, and breathe out any tension.

When you're steady in his presence, ask him (while focusing on the quiet, steady thoughts he brings into your mind instead of the broken record of your inner critic):

Am I living under "dark rumors" or lies now? If so, what are they, Jesus?

_____

_____

_____

What do I most often criticize about myself?

_____

_____

Read Romans 8:12–14 from *The Message* slowly:

"So don't you see that we don't owe this old do-it-yourself life one red cent. There's nothing in it for us, nothing at all. The best thing to do is give it a decent burial and get on with your new life. God's Spirit beckons. There are things to do and places to go!"

Prayerfully ask the Lord what, if anything, from your old nature needs to be given a decent burial.

Ask him to show you how you and he can bury this today:

_____

_____

What practical difference would it make in your life to be assured that you have a completely new nature to live in, that your old nature of fear, doubt, sin, and anxiety has been rendered obsolete? What would need to change in your thinking in order to "get on with your new life"? In your feelings?

_____

_____

Place your awareness solidly on the person of Christ as he is next to and inside you. Ask him what specifically in your new life he wants you to get going on.

_____

_____

Prayerfully ask him what he wants your takeaway to be from this chapter.

_____

Now listen to song #5 in the "*Savor*, the Book" playlist as you revel in the truth expressed.

6

SELF-IMAGE: SPIRIT
OR FALLEN?

THROUGHOUT SONG OF SOLOMON THE KING RAVES,

"O most *beautiful* among women" (1:8).

"You are *beautiful*, my love" (1:15).

"Arise, my love, my *beautiful* one, and come away" (2:13).

"Your lips are [red]; your mouth is [*beautiful*]" (4:3).

"You're *beautiful* from head to toe" (4:7 MSG).

"You are *beautiful* as Tirza, my love" (6:4). (Italics added in the preceding six Scripture quotes are used for emphasis.)

You get the picture. She's *hot!*—even though she hates anyone to look at her.

The king's words aren't flattery; he's not just trying to be encouraging. He never lies. What he sees is her actual "spirit/Spirit" self—her true "in-Jesus" self—if you will, and it's beautiful. Is she still dark? Probably. But in the language of the gospel of Christ, the darkness has been done away with. His focus for the Shulamite, as with us, is on the entirely new person who has been born in her and now lives in the newness of Jesus.

Notice that his words about her beauty directly counter her core lie that she's dark and ugly. His messages to us are custom-tailored to the places where our lies and rumors reside. (For some who don't resonate with Jesus saying, "You're beautiful," he might say, "You're honored; so honorable." "You're respected.") His words shape our self-image into who we actually are in the Spirit.

He Delights in Us Today

The king reiterates (embarrassingly!) his delight in the Shulamite. He simply loves to look at her and say what he sees. He loves to delight in us as well and custom-tailors experiences that he can share with us.

A friend who loves to cook (she's an amazing cook who conjures the most interesting and delectable combos and textures of flavors and foods you could ever imagine) recently shared with me a vision the Lord gave her. She had been meditating on Luke 12:35–38 (ESV) about being ready when the Lord returns when this sentence stood out: "Truly, I say to you, he will dress himself for service and have them recline at table, and he will come and serve them." She suddenly had a picture in her mind's eye in which Jesus showed up at her front door holding a huge rack of lamb (shaped like a crown) to cook for her, with the biggest smile and belly laugh. He said, "Look what I brought you! Wait until you taste this! Sit down. Let me cook for you." Then he told her how glad he was to see her. She said she felt deep attachment to him, joy and gratitude. There's a lot of symbolism in this vision, which she's continuing to unpack. It is a powerful picture of mutual delight surrounding her love language—involving food! (If he showed up with a rack of lamb in my vision, I'd say, "Huh?" I'm not a lamb fan and not into cooking in general. He constantly asks me to dance with him, though!)

Some of us love to study; Jesus comes as a teacher and at times as a fellow learner, pointing out and getting excited about fresh revelations he shares with us. Some love to work with their hands; he draws near and enjoys watching with delight what's taking shape under our fingers. Some love movies and popcorn; you guessed it—he plops down next to us with the bowl.

Recall the last time you enjoyed the Lord . . . a time you felt close to him, sensing or hearing his words to you. What was the context? How did you feel at that time?

What made it enjoyable?

Going deeper, was this experience custom-tailored to your personality? What message do you think he wants you to grasp from this experience?

He Helps Navigate a Fallen Self-image

Recently I allowed a cloud of worthlessness to invade my headspace. I was comparing myself to another spiritual director and coming up short. I became a little jealous and depressed. I mucked about in self-pity and hurt for a bit but then reflected on my feelings, using my usual formula to figure out my struggle:

1. What's the lie? *That I'm a "nothing"—worthless.*

2. What's the vow or strategy I've employed to beat this lie? *I look to people for affirmation or confirmation of who I am, and if I don't get it (and get it in HD), I believe I'm junk. I compare to make myself feel value.*

3. How's this strategy been working for me? *It brings the fruit of darkness and self-absorption. Yuck!*

In my struggle I opened up to Jesus, telling him in detail how I was feeling, complete with emotion words from the feelings wheel (*rejected, insecure, insignificant* and *inadequate*). Because "I'm worthless" is a core lie of mine, I've brought this same experience to him on multiple occasions in the past but with different details. I waited, sensing his support, his understanding, his extreme patience, and his love.

After a bit, he nodded and said, "Oh, yeah. I've seen all that." He then flicked his fingers as though he were getting rid of some little gnat, that is, he flicked away my lie, my strategy. . . . (Oh, the *years* this has been my M.O). Then he said, looking into my eyes with love so great it took my breath away, "But *you're mine!*"

Just like that, it all evaporated—the lie, the cloud of darkness. My strategy to compare (trying to shore up my own sense of worthlessness) deflated like a popped balloon, simply with a flick of his wrist and his assertion of "You're mine."

The perfect love of Jesus expels darkness once again. Deep inhale of the rarified air of the gospel!

Selah

Take some deep breaths as you settle your mind. If it's helpful, recall the inner room/holy place you saw or felt from the *Selah* reflections of chapter 3. Enter that place again in your imagination and simply relax there.

Jesus is the way, the truth, and the life (see John 14:6). With each deep inhale, breathe in these aspects of him. "See" him opening the way to truth for you now as you consider the following:

Think for a moment about your core lie (where your rumors most often come from). What is it?

Look at the picture[14] above.

Imagine you are the cub. How do you feel walking around this desert as just you, yourself—a cub?

Now imagine what the picture expresses: you are still you, but the image of your father lion shines out through your "cub-ness" for all to see. Is there a difference in how you feel walking around now? In how you see yourself?

_____

_____

Is there a message from the Lord to you in this scene?

_____

Now take some additional deep breaths. Settle into the gaze of Christ within your spirit. His gaze can present as his *face* with eyes reflecting understanding and support. Or his gaze can come as a *feeling* of being seen, known. Let this gaze become real to you; don't move on until you sense his presence seeing you.

When you sense his gaze, ask him how he sees you. What delights him about you?

_____

Rest for a minute in your actual "spirit/Spirit self"—the beautiful, strong, pure, loving person Jesus sees when he looks at you. Rest in the self who makes him say, "Turn away your eyes from me, for they overwhelm me" (Song of Solomon 6:5). This is the new creation of you—of me—after the old you has been crucified.

What difference would it make to you if his image of you would be your own constant self-image, if you were to see yourself as the strong, stunning person whom Jesus sees and loves? He's admiring his own handiwork after all.

How would your life be different? Consider emotions, behaviors.

_____

_____

Close your time in reflection by listening to song #6 in the "*Savor*, the Book" playlist.

7

GUILT

D ID YOU NOTICE? The Shulamite is the only one who mentions her darkness, and only in a few verses in the first chapter. After that, the darkness is not mentioned again. The king doesn't even deem it worthy of comment! The Shulamite could have asked forgiveness, but she didn't. She might have felt the need to apologize to the king for being a slave to the sons of her mother but of another father, but this doesn't come out in the narrative. Operating under the old nature when we don't realize there's an alternative doesn't necessitate "repentance," according to the Song of Solomon. But what about when we know better, when we do what we know we shouldn't?

A sense of shame ("I'm bad") is never from God. Guilt ("I've done bad") can be the conviction of the Spirit, although it comes with such gentleness that we end up thanking and worshiping him. There's never condemnation or accusation with legitimate guilt that comes from God—condemnation is from the accuser. So when we've behaved or spoken in ways we know are wrong, how do we respond?

We respond the same as throughout this guide: we bring all of it to Jesus—bring him the feelings of shame, the guilt, the excuses and justifications, the anger, and the underneath feelings that anger is protecting. Talk out all of the emotion as he patiently listens. When we're through with our words, we ask him what's going on within us or around us that prompted these actions or words. For a new-creation Christian, things we do or say that bring legitimate guilt are simply stepping stones toward further healing and freedom as we receive truth and life from the Spirit.

There are good lessons to be learned, and fresh truths about Jesus, self, or others that contribute toward our growth and closeness to God.

Truly, redemption = sin becoming positive.

The "Examen"

The spiritual exercise of *examen* is helpful here. The *examen* simply brings the events of the previous day (practice this exercise either in the evening or first thing in the morning) to the Spirit for his search. We ask—

> Where did I most sense your presence and closeness during this day?
> Where did I seem to lose the sense of your presence?
> What do you want to show me from this day?

Then we wait for him to bring to our remembrance scenes or reminders from the day. We play prayer-tennis with him, asking questions, responding emotionally and cognitively, serving the ball back to him. We receive what he brings us. Practicing the *examen* daily sharpens our awareness of truth and deepens intimacy with him.

The *examen* can be tailored to whatever you'd like it to be. For instance, asking more specifically, "Where did I feel anxiety today?" or "When did I sense my arrogance or pride showing itself?" can help pinpoint where the Spirit is working in us. Keeping it more positive, we can ask him, "At what time today did I feel the most like myself, relaxed and free?" Mirror your *examen* to reflect wherever you are on the intimacy journey.

During an *examen* we position ourselves to receive what the Spirit of Christ wants to show us; it is an exercise of leaning back with an open heart, focusing our love and attention on the Lord and all he's given us. This, however, is *not* a time of soul excavation, digging through memories of the day under the harsh leadership of our inner critic.

If this exercise comes with accusation, darkness, a sense of futility, or dark depression, this is not from God. There is great compassion and help for this kind of inner turmoil; I know from experience. (You may benefit from counseling, therapy, spiritual direction, deliverance, or medication. I encourage you to seek help if you experience repeated bouts of darkness.)

Selah—Prayer Experience of Examen

Slow your breathing; sink into your chair; the "everlasting arms" are beneath you, holding you up. Breathe slowly until the peace of Christ envelops you. Sense his love, his delight in you.

The *examen:*

Where have I sensed the Spirit's presence and communication most clearly this past twenty-four hours?

_____

_____

During this past day, where did Jesus seem to withdraw?

_____

_____

Are there any words or behaviors you want to talk with me about, Jesus?

_____

_____

When you're ready, listen to song #7 in the "*Savor,* the Book" playlist.

8

REST

T HE SHULAMITE, RECOGNIZING THAT HER "OLD NATURE" BEHAVIORS ARE RESULTING IN EXHAUSTION AND A BAD SUNBURN, HAS JUST ASKED THE KING WHERE HE GRAZES HIS SHEEP AT NOON. She's beginning to want his leadership, not that of her old-nature brothers!

He answers in Song of Solomon 1:8 (TPT), "Listen, my radiant one—if you ever lose sight of me, just follow in my footsteps where I lead my lovers. Come with your burdens and cares. Come to the place near the sanctuary of my shepherds."

My paraphrase: "If you want to find me, **come to where you are shepherded— where you can rest, where you receive nourishment.** This is where you'll find me. I'm never harsh; I'll never drive you to exhaustion. I don't motivate you by fear, guilt, or shame. You can bring your responsibilities and busy life to this green pasture, always and whenever you need. Let me apply the gospel to your struggle. You'll find me here."

The gospel—Jesus dying for us so that our sin and old nature are rendered powerless—can become so familiar that we don't often revel in the grandeur of it. Song of Solomon presents a beautiful picture of how to live under this grace and love: "As the king surrounded me at his table, the sweet fragrance of spikenard awakened the night" (Song of Solomon 1:12 TPT).

Let's consider this next scene in our story: the Shulamite and king are enjoying a meal together. She sniffs appreciatively; it's not a food smell, although delicious food is present. It's a sweet, desirable smell, but coming from where? She suddenly realizes it's coming from her! The one who by her own words is dark, working all day in the heat . . . by implication, she's smelly! But no—this beautiful smell is emanating from her.

The Gospel Protects Us

She looks down. Surprisingly she sees a sachet of myrrh sitting right over her heart. "A sachet of myrrh is my lover, like a tied-up bundle of myrrh resting over my heart" (1:13 TPT).

Myrrh: a spice used in embalming oil. It carries the meaning of death, a reminder of the death of Jesus. Myrrh was also part of the recipe for anointing oil.

Over her heart: Myrrh doesn't need to be over her head, or by inference, over our heads. We already know cognitively that Jesus saves, forgives, and cleanses us. Rather, it sits guard over her heart and our *hearts*, the seat of emotion, the gut place of our "knower." We know that we know . . . this is our heart. The Bible used to translate this idea as the kidneys: the seat of temperament, emotions, and wisdom. Eclipsing our mental thoughts, the death and resurrection of Jesus protect this emotional seat of our being. With iron-clad certainty, the gospel protects my freedom to revel in my own goodness, honor, and beauty as God's transforming child.

I am new! I am clean! Quiet your cognition and simply "feel the feels."

This thought of Jesus being our protector from our old nature continues in the next verse: "My beloved is to me a cluster of henna blossoms in the vineyards of Engedi" (1:14). Henna plants are thorny bushes with fragrant flowers. Because of their dense prickliness, they were planted around vineyards in order to keep predators from entering and eating the fruit. The Lord here assures us of his love and protection as we cultivate our inner garden, this vineyard of our relationship with him. He has done everything to ensure the beautiful, pleasing, emotionally satisfying relationship of love and intimacy with him.

Dove's Eyes

The king, realizing the Shulamite is starting to smell her own fragrance of goodness, now erupts with joy as he exclaims, "Oh, how beautiful! Your eyes are doves!" (1:15). Paraphrased: "You're starting to look at yourself with the eyes of the Holy Spirit! You see your true spirit-self!"

Within the embrace of Jesus's love, we remember his death for us and his power. Having put to death all the rumors and lies of our old nature, we allow him to create a Holy Spirit image of ourselves. We receive this image as we tune in to his words of affirmation. We gradually start to agree with him, and our personal dove's eyes become clear and focused.

Song of Solomon chapter 1 ends with the Shulamite and the king relaxing in a shady, green, fragrant place. She's resting because she's starting to see herself through the eyes of the Holy Spirit, whose gift to us is rest. The king is resting because he's reveling in her fragrance and in this fresh relationship that's budding between them.

If the foundation of our intimacy is the completed work of the cross, then the atmosphere and opening to intimacy is rest.

Selah

Deep breaths. Calm your mind and body. Imagine a shady, green place of rest. You may want to imagine a forest, a beach—wherever you feel rested and refreshed.

What does it look like in your mind's eye?

_____

Is there a breeze or a particular fragrance?

_____

Enjoy and savor for a moment. (Lingering within a sense of peace or rest is important for neuroplasticity—the rewiring of our neural pathways—in our brains.)

Is this sensation of mental, physical, and emotional rest with Jesus your usual vibe as you go about your day? Is it sometimes? Or never?

_____

Our "Holy Spirit eyes" grow by becoming aware of our king's words of affirmation to us. Ask him, from a place of rest and listening, to write you some of those affirmations now. Record them as if he were writing them to you:

My loved and honored one, what I see in you is . . .

_____

_____

_____

_____

Hearing his words of affirmation is one thing. Choosing to agree with him is another. Are you agreeing with him?

_____

As you believe what he thinks of you, how does your self-image shift? How should it shift?

_____

Listen to song #8 in the "*Savor, the Book*" playlist. Listen to the lyrics and receive the Spirit's inner workings in you.

9

A HOUSE OF WINE

AS IS THE CASE WITH MOST SATISFYING JOURNEYS, ELEMENTS OF REST, FUN, AND RELAXATION MINGLE WITH SURPRISE, ADVENTURE, AND TWISTS. The Shulamite's journey is no different.

Momentary Doubt

Our heroine has been relaxing in the green coolness of her king's words. She's reveling in her newfound fragrance. In a word, she's *savoring* . . . until she's not.

Song of Solomon 2:1–2 (MSG):

> Her: I'm just a wildflower picked from the plains of Sharon, a lotus blossom from the valley pools.
>
> Him: A lotus blossoming in a swamp of weeds—that's my dear friend among the girls in the village.

The Hebrew word for *lotus blossom* (or "rose of Sharon") isn't actually very elegant. It's possibly a word for *crocus,* something that grows wild and is common.

So to paraphrase, she starts thinking, "Hmm—I have a fragrance but it's nothing really. I'm just a dandelion—that's all. One of millions."

Do we also start to waver? You bet. I do for sure. We evaluate, compare, come up short . . . and our old nature mindset comes roaring back. It's somehow encouraging to see the Shulamite do the same thing.

These waverings can actually be positive in that they indicate to us where we still have places within us that aren't healed. The familiar lies and arrows the enemy hits us with are like a spotlight from Jesus saying, "Look at this! Bring this area to me and let's heal it!"

How does the king respond to the Shulamite? By giving her his gift of preferring her above others. Paraphrased: "Actually, you're the best! I'm the only one qualified to compare you, and I see your spirit-self. I see that it's beautiful, honorable, and so sweet-smelling!"

Surviving her momentary doubt, she sits down under his shade and the story continues.

Relaxation and the Wine of God

Song of Solomon 2:3–6 (NCV):

> Among the young men, my lover is like an apple tree in the woods! I enjoy sitting in his shadow; his fruit is sweet to my taste. He brought me to the banquet room, and his banner over me is love. Strengthen me with raisins, and refresh me with apples, because I am weak with love. My lover's left hand is under my head, and his right arm holds me tight.

Satisfied by the king's preference of her, she returns to resting in his shade, eating his fruit. This picture of nourishment and rest is the primary realm for our deep growth of intimacy. He feeds us. We eat. We rest. We share our feelings and thoughts, holding nothing back from our king. We receive his heart, his feelings, his laughter, his words and pictures. We respond. Repeat.

In current phraseology, we are *attuning* to our Father.

Centering prayer (covered in the next chapter) is helpful here. This kind of prayer creates neural pathways of present-moment living, and intimacy with Christ always occurs in the present moment. Picture intimacy with Jesus like swimming in an ocean—wherever I swim he's there, all needs met (present moment). Being anxious or fearful is usually future-oriented. Anxiety tosses me out onto the beach as I gasp for air. Jesus comes and scoops me up, putting me back into the ocean, where I can breathe again. Needs and longings are met in the present moment.

Returning to the narrative, the king transports the Shulamite to the house of wine. It's not a "banqueting table," as some Bible versions translate it. The original translation is "house of wine" that is, a place to drink wine (whose purpose according to Psalm 104:15 is to gladden human hearts). Do we picture this about our God—that he brings us to places intended simply to relax us and make us glad?

Selah

Again, deep breaths. Savor the word picture from this chapter of resting in his shade. He shields us from the hot sun of the world, the enemy, and our old nature like a huge, green tree on a beautiful summer day.

Imagine yourself, sitting with the Lord under his shade. You're relaxing, nibbling on tidbits of food, either natural or supernatural. You and he are enjoying yourselves; your heart is glad. You laugh together, maybe share a joke or two. In your sanctified imagination, how does this shady place look? What elements are here? What do you smell? Is there a breeze? Stay here a moment.

_____

_____

_____

Now suddenly you are in a different place. It's like the local pub or brewery. Jesus stands to your side; you realize there's a big sign over your head that reads "LOVED" (or you can imagine a different word he'd write over you: "Mine" or "Honored"). How do you experience being in this scene?

_____

_____

As you see this "house of wine" scene in your mind's eye, what else is in the picture? Is it a noisy or quiet place? Are other people present or not? If so, do you recognize any faces?

_____

_____

_____

Now look over at Jesus standing near you. What does his face look like to you? What do his eyes convey? What's his general vibe? Jot down anything you want to remember:

_____

_____

_____

Listen to song #9 in the "*Savor*, the Book" playlist; take in the words and feel their truth.

10

CENTERING PRAYER AND THE SILENCE OF GOD

A MINOR HICCUP OCCURS NEXT IN THE STORY. In Song of Solomon 2:5 the Shulamite is so faint with love for her king that she sighs, "Food! Raisins! I want something nourishing to eat!" But this time he doesn't feed her; he embraces her instead. This is the first time in the tableau when he actually hugs her in a definitely loving and intimate embrace.

What's the hiccup here? We sometimes long for something from the Word, some cognitive thought or truth to sustain us. Our primary spiritual education comes from Scripture as we read, study, meditate, and receive insight from the Holy Spirit. But sometimes we get nothing cognitive; he offers us a silence that can be unnerving.

Realize in these silent times that he's communicating all right—he's actually bringing something far more intimate than a nourishing tidbit of truth: his embrace. Intimacy and maturity deepen when we resist the urge to figure out what we've done wrong to merit his silence and instead sink deeply into the quiet, all-encompassing embrace of love itself.

His silence is an invitation to go deeper, to surrender cares both good and bad, and to release attachment to things, circumstances, or people. Understand his silence as beckoning us to experience his person in ways that are farther in and deeper down. When the prodigal son returned in Luke 15, his father said not one word to him verbally. But he showed his immense love by running toward him and showering him with gifts. How does the Father show his love to you through actions alone?

Consider that his silence can also be indicative of our stiff-arming him, or disobedience to what he's impressed upon us to do.

How does this idea of Jesus embracing you—in a way that's more than a quick side hug—hit you? His embrace can conjure all kinds of "bad" reactions, bad because of our upbringing perhaps, or what we've been taught about God. (He's holy! We must hide our base instincts from him!)

It's really important in the quest for deep intimacy not to stop the process here out of fear or by stuffing down legitimate reactions. Bring to Jesus everything you feel, sense, or desire as you picture being embraced by Jesus. Put words to it. Use descriptive adjectives; how does this idea of his strong, deep love make you feel? What does it bring up about your perception of him? If this feels creepy or wrong, explore where these feelings and reactions come from. Explore with him, that is.

Our bodies and being are made in his image; he truly understands, loves, and accepts all that we are and all that we bring to him because he is exactly *like us* in our humanity. Rest here in the perfect no-condemnation presence of Jesus, who loves our every part and who longs to heal the broken parts with his love.

Record your feelings and any words or thoughts you have now, resting in his embrace.

_____

_____

_____

_____

_____

Good Advice

At precisely this point, the witnesses insert the following advice: "Oh, let me warn you, sisters in Jerusalem, by the gazelles, yes, by all the wild deer: Don't excite love, don't stir it up, until the time is ripe—and you're ready" (Song of Solomon 2:7 MSG).

This is a timely bit of mentoring . . . we set the pace as our king leads us.

Centering Prayer

Intrinsic to our experience of intimacy with Jesus and our ability to rest in him, even and especially when he is silent, is the ability to quiet our brains. Hands-down, the practice of centering prayer[15] has been the single most important prayer practice for ushering me into deeper experiences of the love of Christ.

Centering prayer began in the dark mists of centuries past but has been making a comeback in recent years. The practice involves simply sitting in the presence of God in a comfortable position, but not one that will induce sleep. We sit with no agenda other than to *be* with Christ. There's no question we are asking, no help we require. This is a gift we give him—our time and simple attention. This kind of prayer leads us from communicating to or with the Lord to a deeper, nonverbal *communion* with him. The length of time we spend is up to us, but twenty minutes twice a day is what we aim for eventually.

At the outset we'll likely encounter "monkey brain" or pinballing thoughts. To counter this, we ask the Lord to give us a *sacred word,* a word he places in our thoughts that, when we gently repeat this word silently to ourselves, will bring our awareness back from our thoughts to the centering place of his presence.

I have been given two sacred words so far: *release* and *retreat.* Friends have shared these words: *love, mercy, peace,* and *Hineni* (a Hebrew phrase meaning "Here I am"). It could also be a short phrase, but no more than two or three words.

At the start of my practice, I couldn't go ten seconds without my thoughts barging in; some days I couldn't go even that long. But I persisted. Neural pathways in my brain seem to be changing; quiet awareness of God is now restful. Mysteriously, tasks on my to-do list get done with no hurried effort, despite giving this exercise extra minutes in the morning and/or evening. Self-control comes easier. The practice of centering prayer benefits literally all avenues of life. . . . So let's try it.

Selah

Get comfortable. Begin with deep breathing for a bit. Center your awareness on Jesus, who's right there with you. As your thoughts come in, don't react to them and don't latch on to them—just gently bring your attention back to God.

In preparation for the centering prayer exercise, listen to song #10 in the "*Savor, the Book*" playlist. Rest in this God.

Ask him to give you a sacred word. You can record it if you'd like:

_____

As thoughts enter, repeat this sacred word and bring your attention back to Jesus. This is not a *concentration* exercise; rather, it's an *awareness* one. Speak your word out loud or in your mind and allow it to relax you and bring you back to him.

It can be helpful to picture your invading thoughts as clouds in the sky. Allow them just to float on by as you refrain from giving them attention.

Or experience centering prayer as if you were sitting on the ocean floor. You are human but have the ability to breathe like a fish. As you sit comfortably, you see shadowy boats going by on the surface—these represent your thoughts—but you simply let them float by as you sit surrounded by the beauty and gentle rhythm of the ocean.

Begin this practice with two minutes in the morning and then two minutes in the evening before bed. It can be frustrating—just persist in it, and amazing benefits will be yours! Gradually increase the practice until you can comfortably do twenty minutes per time, or as much as you feel helps you. The Lord will bend the time in your day to get everything else done in peace and with ease.

Record anything you learn about yourself or about God from this prayer exercise.

_____

_____

_____

_____

_____

_____

11

THE REAL JOURNEY

THE DEEPER OUR INTIMACY WITH JESUS, THE MORE COMPLETE OUR HEALING WILL BE. This is because gazing at his glory by receiving his words of love and affirmation begins to shift and lessen our shame, brokenness, and wounding. We discover our darkness taking a back seat to newfound pleasure and peace as old-nature inner messages are replaced with the love messages of our beloved.

The perfect love found in intimacy with Christ literally displaces fear, shame, and anxiety; it heals wounds and realigns neural pathways in our brain. As we allow him to, Jesus rewrites our narratives of the past with fresh perspective. Forget self-help plans! Love—and our being able to experience this passionate, sweetly longing, always-gentle-while-being-strong-and-commanding love of Jesus—this is truly the answer to the many inner struggles we have. But it comes at a price. The price is a long surrender in the right direction, a coming out of hiding, a risk-taking trust in the one who calls us "Beloved."

The Song of Solomon begins to hint at this part of the journey in chapter 2. The king is pleading with the Shulamite as she sits behind a wall. Note the urgency she recounts for us from the king's words to her:

Song of Solomon 2:8–11, 13–14:

> Her: The voice of my beloved! Behold, he comes, leaping over the mountains, bounding over the hills. . . . Behold, there he stands behind our wall, gazing through the windows, looking through the lattice.

My beloved speaks and says to me: "Arise, my love, my beautiful one, and come away, for behold, the winter is past; the rain is over and gone. . . . Arise, my love, my beautiful one, and come away. O my dove, in the clefts of the rock, in the crannies of the cliff, let me see your face, let me hear your voice, for your voice is sweet, and your face is lovely."

The king is announcing a fresh season for the Shulamite and asking her to come out, to "arise" and come with him. He's leaping and bounding—can you sense his excitement? King Jesus, running around like a deer, leaping with joy? The long cold winter is now over, he proclaims. It's time to get up and come away with him to a place yet unspecified. He's excited for this—finally she's understanding the life-changing importance of his sacrifice on the cross for her. She's beginning to cease from her frantic striving to please him and others; she's learning the sweetness of being loved and accepting that love. She even likes it. Passionately. He's excited!

But . . . she's not yet ready.

Walls

She's "behind the wall." He must "gaze through the windows, look through the lattice." They're separated, although he can see everything. In another metaphor he implores her to come away from the cliff face and allow him to see her face, hear her voice. In spite of her lolling around in his shade, eating his succulent fruit, she now hides from him. And she quiets her voice.

Note that he doesn't come behind the wall to literally carry her out. Sometimes that's what we want him to do: "Can't you just wave a magic wand and help me get over this, Jesus?" No, this next part in the story requires her cooperation. She must unlock the door herself (see Song of Solomon 5:4). She also must come out from behind the places where she hides.

In our journey of deepening intimacy with Christ, we will each be faced with different choices. This is what makes the journey hard—and usually the best choice will include a death of something. But having choices allows our love response to Jesus to be free, never coerced.

At the end of the king's beautiful words of invitation above ("Come out! Let's go to the heights! I have things to show you and you're gonna love it!"), he slides in a surprising comment that stops her cold.

Foxes

Song of Solomon 2:15: "Catch the foxes for us, the little foxes that spoil the vineyards, for our vineyards are in blossom."

Paraphrased:

> Beloved, I see some intruders have gotten past the protective fence I made for your vineyard; they're fairly small but can do a lot of damage if left untended. Actually, they'll pretty much ruin this intimate relationship we're building here if not dealt with, so let's take care of them. What do you say?

She answers:

> Until the day springs to life and the shifting shadows of fear disappear, turn around, my lover, and ascend to the holy mountains of separation without me. Until the new day fully dawns, run on ahead. . . . Go on ahead to the mountain of spices—I'll come away another time. (Song of Solomon 2:17 TPT)

The original Hebrew is "mountains of Bether"; *Bether* means separation. In essence she reacts in this way to his bringing up her foxes: "Umm, no! Don't you get all up in my foxes! Those are *my* foxes, and I don't want you to *touch them*! You can just go your way now; leave me be."

Perhaps that's a bit too strong. Trying again . . . paraphrased:

> Okay, Jesus. Now really isn't the time. Maybe when I'm not so fearful, maybe after a new day dawns . . . after (fill in the blank: *I get another job, my kids are raised, I make more money and am not so tired, after* . . .), then I'll deal with the foxes. But for now, you go—you go to your mountain and I'll stay here on mine. Good night.

In our journey with Jesus we meet these kinds of places of separation. He puts his finger on something in our lives. Maybe it's something in our repeated dreams at night; perhaps it's an issue that others have pointed out. Maybe it's the *something* that's on your mind right now.

Reflect back on the foxes in verse 2. They are spoiling the vineyard. What metaphor do foxes represent?

In Scripture there is not even one positive image of a fox or a jackal; even Samson's foxes with their tails tied together and on fire did great damage to fields. For our purposes, foxes can be distractions, habits that aren't the healthiest. They can be old patterns of response that served us well back in the day but now need to be refreshed. Foxes might be as simple as disobedience to God's still, small voice, a disobedience that we assume won't matter.

Characteristics of foxes in vineyards:

- They're small; they look insignificant but over time can do great damage.

- They gnaw the vines off at the ground, causing the out-of-reach fruit to fall with the ruined vine.

- Some common foxes: Bitterness. Unforgiveness. Shame. Fear. Anxiety. Lust.

- Allowing foxes to remain means we are in essence saying *no* to intimacy. We stiff-arm God. Then intimacy slows down or even stops.

At this point we each have a choice to make: we can courageously deal with the fox with Jesus's help and love—remember the henna hedge he already has in place to protect us as we deal with it—or we can leave the fox for now.

A Tale of Two Women

Once upon a time there were two elderly women. Jesus loved them; both were believers in Christ for most of their lives. One lived in trusting obedience to her Lord, to the people around her, and although she readily confessed her fears as she became old and infirm, she continued to say, "I just trust the Lord."

The other woman attended church and helped many people during her life. But she consistently turned down invitations to join Bible studies and prayer meetings. She believed in doing things herself and refused to open up to others about needs in her life. She ignored the still, small voice of God. She spent her life stiff-arming invitations to deeper intimacy from the Lord.

Although Jesus loved and took care of each woman during her lifetime on earth, the first passed very peacefully, and many grieved her death. The second fought to keep control of everything in her life, becoming difficult emotionally and socially as the end drew near. Although she attended church, she had never learned to trust God. Fear imprisoned her as she aged.

It may be hard to understand the full physiological and emotional reasons for the difference in the two women, but the issue of relying on God vs. relying on self surely played a part. The end of our lives will tell the tale of how we dealt with our foxes and fears.

In the Shulamite's story, she decided to leave the fox. Let's see how that worked out for her in the next chapter.

Selah

Deeply breathe. Settle underneath the shade of Jesus and relax your mind and body. There's no false guilt, condemnation, and no accusation of self or anyone else. Relax with the shepherd. Sense his love reaching out for you now.

Tune in to your thoughts and feelings. Be honest with any adjectives or feelings you now have after reading this chapter. What's on your mind?

_____

_____

Is there an area of your life you're wishing the Lord would just wave a magic wand and fix? This might be something you hide from. If so, what is it?

_____

Listen to song #11 in the "*Savor, the Book*" playlist before continuing. Consider the amazing truth from this song about the need to go through tough places instead of being rescued from them by the Lord.

Looking at the picture[16] above, feel the chewing of this fox.

Ask, "Jesus, is there a fox in my vineyard that's ruining my intimacy with you? What is this fox's name?

_____

"As I gaze at you and your glory, how can we deal with this fox?"

_____

_____

Recall the scene at the start of this chapter; the king implores the Shulamite to "come away, for the winter is past; the rain is over and gone. . .a time of singing has come." This beckoning to a fresh season of joy is the reason he needs her to come out of hiding, to deal with the foxes.

As you rest in the peace and love of Christ, ask him what winter season is past or might soon be past for you.

Is there a season of singing he's longing to bring you into now? As you quiet your mind, allow him to tell you about this coming season, in Immanuel Journaling:

My child, I want to bring you into a season of . . .

_____

_____

_____

_____

_____

_____

12

DARK NIGHT OF THE SOUL

PERHAPS YOU'VE HEARD THE PHRASE *THE DARK NIGHT OF THE SOUL*. This is a concept first expressed by sixteenth-century Spanish monk St. John of the Cross, who wrote about the interior life with Christ. His poetry describes the concept that later came to be known as *the dark night of the soul* or "the active and passive purification of the senses and the spirit."[17] A dark night season is characterized by *the suspension of our sensing awareness* of the Lord, by a general dryness spiritually. Worship ceases to move us as it used to. Scripture holds little interest. Fellowship with other Christians seems tiresome, and we feel alone. The only desire we might feel is a simple attraction to rest, to be alone, mildly aware of God in his seeming emptiness. These times can go on for weeks, months, or years. Some common responses to a dark night of the soul are—

- *What did I do wrong?* We begin soul excavation to try to figure this out.

- *I'm going to memorize more verses, read more books, pray harder—strive to get into his good graces again.* This can actually help in a limited way until we wear out from exhaustion.

- *I guess he's not interested in me.* We turn away from or "deconstruct" faith, in part or in whole, with resentment disguised as resignation.

Such reactions are actually important parts of the journey. The pain we experience with each fresh unanswered prayer or each time of silence from God chips away at the strong self-will we might not even know is operating. "I'm just trying to do the will of God!" we sigh, not realizing he doesn't want or need our work. He wants our surrender, trust, and relationship.

Purpose of Dark Nights

Dark nights help wean us from the comforts of his felt presence, ushering in deeper maturity in Christ and communion with the Spirit. Dark nights can reveal our weakness (weakness is a positive in God's economy) and enable us to thirst for the person of Christ rather than his gifts.

Dark nights are an invitation to something deeper, more personal with God, less general. Striving is exposed; hiding places are stripped. Dark nights of the soul reach deeply into places of pain where we huddle behind a wall of self-protection. During these nights, striving gradually quiets into surrender and rest. While we might feel forsaken by God, he's right there in every detail and moment . . . watching, caring, holding our hearts and keeping them from breaking. With hindsight we can trace his every move and realize the exquisite love that has tracked us.

The Shulamite's first dark night is rather straightforward: she had stiff-armed the king. She had told him to go to his mountain without her, and he did. Now she seeks him but can't find him. She feels his absence keenly; she's distressed. And more, it's at night, when things can be distorted anyway. Song of Solomon 3:1: "On my bed by night I sought him whom my soul loves; I sought him but found him not."

Lying there in the dark isn't helping, so she gets up. "I will rise now and go about the city, in the streets and in the squares; I will seek him whom my soul loves. I sought him but found him not. The watchmen found me as they went about in the city. 'Have you seen him whom my soul loves?'" (Song of Solomon 3:2–3).

Note that she gets up—what he was asking her to do in chapter 2—and heads to the city, looking for him. She's desperate. The dark night of her soul is working, purifying her soul and senses.

But wait! In chapter one the king tells her that if she can't find him, she's to go to the fields. He instructs her to go where she feels shepherded, where there's plenty of nourishing green grass, where she can find others who will help her reconnect with him again. So . . . what's she doing in the city? Indeed, that's the question.

Cities We Run To

The word *city* in Hebrew is a "fortified place" and can carry a sense of excitement—or a sense of terror. This running to something exciting when I really need intimacy with my shepherd is a behavior I identify with. Somehow going into a place of rest, greenery, and nourishment to relax and connect with Jesus can seem boring (or some other emotion), and I instead seek an interesting or exciting outlet to revive me. The "cities" we run to can be destructive or innocent, but when intimacy with the king is our need, the noise and excitement of a city actually deadens the very thirst we have for him and hastens a downward counterproductive spiral.

What cities do you typically run to? Pause and consider.

The Shulamite is about to get a deep experience of the gospel's grace and width in what happens next. Song of Solomon 3:4: "Scarcely had I passed them when I found him whom my soul loves. I held him and would not let him go until I had brought him into my mother's house, and into the chamber of her who conceived me."

Rather than waiting for her in some far-off green field, tapping his foot impatiently, her king is right here, smack in the middle of her city! This is the grace of the gospel in action. Our king pursues us; he doesn't wait until we get our act together. He's not somewhere off shaking his finger, saying, "I *told* you. . . ." Our man attracts to our need—whatever it is at the moment—like a magnet. Exquisite closeness. Deep compassion. Embrace of love.

The king says nothing when the Shulamite finds him; he just opens his arms, and she runs into them. The Passion Translation phrases it, "I caught him and fastened myself to him." The Message: "I threw my arms around him and held him tight." We *cleave* to him. We sag against him in relief.

This is the first mention of her initiating a hug. As she experiences the deep and complete grace of the gospel—devoid of any condemnation or accusation—her trust in her king expands and elevates like a hot air balloon. The intimacy between them leaps into the stratosphere as she experiences him in the *city*, searching and waiting for her. Imagine her relief that he's not mad at her for stiff-arming him. She says to herself, "*He's here! He really doesn't condemn me for turning away! I can trust this kind of love. Okay, I'm gonna go out on a limb and say that my entire life— from when my mother conceived me until this point—is now 'open season' to him. Foxes, walls. . . whatever he wants to address, I'm in,*" as she clings happily to him.

Note: there's no repentance, no confession of her disobedience. There's no wallowing: "I did it *again*, Lord! How can you even look at me? I'm such a mess. I'm just gonna give up!" I recall a time when I was wallowing like this in my own bad actions, and after a bit the Lord said to me, "Stop. You've just fallen off a pedestal I never put you on. I know who you are and why you do things. Now get up and stop groveling." Boom. I quit wallowing.

Falling more deeply in love with Jesus happens in the murky waters of our shame, our pain, our scars. He can't stay away from our messes; they are his favorite part! He entered our condition when he died; he erased the shame, pain, and scars with his "It is finished." We can let down our guard and allow him to do what he's best at: accept, heal, and transform.

To Be Practical . . .

Have you ever stiff-armed God, avoided something his still, small voice was saying? Flatly refused to go where he wanted you to go relationally, emotionally, or with a memory from the past? Some of us don't flatly refuse; we do a passive thing like telling ourselves we're just too tired or busy. We believe nothing good can come from . . . opening *that* can of worms. When he puts his finger on something, though, he can be pretty insistent. After all, this *thing* we fear addressing is actually a chain around our ankles; it limits intimacy with the only one who gives freedom. And he's a jealous lover who won't just stand back and let us stay chained.

Selah

After taking some deep breaths, relax your body into his quiet presence. Take a bit of time to pull back from the words of this chapter, and allow your awareness to shift to the face and love of the Lord.

When thoughts have quieted, is there anything from this chapter that has risen gently to the surface of your mind? What is it?

_____

_____

Focus on how Jesus seems to you now as he is present beside you.

Now picture this: You're in the "city" of your usual choosing. (Remember: cities can be wonderful places to enjoy with Jesus as part of our unique design, or they can be pits of destruction—but if we are hungry for what only he provides, running here is completely counterproductive.) Be aware of your emotional and bodily response to being in this city. What does your city give you?

_____

_____

Has there been a cost to you or others from your trips to this city?

_____

_____

Now ask the Lord where he is in this city's scene as you picture it in your mind.

When you see him, what do you sense about him; how does he seem to you? If you can see his face, what do his eyes convey? Savor this moment; wait on what he wants to say right now. Record what he gives you:

_____

_____

Are there any thoughts you want to write back to him?

_____

_____

Move further in and notice his response to what you wrote or told him.

_____

_____

When you've completed this reflection with Jesus, listen to song #12 in the "*Savor,* the Book" playlist, as if he were singing it to you.

13

ONE STEP AHEAD

THROUGHOUT THE EIGHT CHAPTERS OF SOLOMON'S SONG WE GLIMPSE Jesus's emotions and personality from the descriptions and actions of the king. This helps us relate with the Spirit of Jesus within. In these chapters the king often seems one step ahead of the Shulamite as her responses to him elicit spontaneous joy.

For example, remember how he let her sit under his shade and eat the love apples for a bit (2:3), but then suddenly—abruptly—he takes her to the house of wine to show her off? Then as she happily sinks into his embrace (after he didn't give her food in 2:5–6), he starts dreaming about the places they'll go and asks her with great urgency to get up and go with him. One step ahead. He's just so excited to see her respond to him.

Think for a moment of the times the Lord has been one step ahead of you. Perhaps he provided a solution before you even knew you had a problem. A parking space appeared before you started looking. You receive affirmation from others right before you hear someone's criticism of your work. A verse you read in the morning applies exactly to a situation in your day.

Recently we stayed for a few days in a mountain cabin. Only on the last morning did I see a mouse running on the very bed I'd been sleeping on. The Lord either kept the mouse away until that last day, or he just prevented me from seeing it while we were there . . . but I took this as a little gift of his concern for squeamish me.

Evidences of his love and awareness are like tiny diamonds from his hands that we can easily miss. He's the master of "coincidence"—it becomes an inside, fun intimacy challenge to watch him sprinkle his jewels of love into our days.

Selah

Quiet your mind and nervous system with some deep breathing. Center your attention on your breath, realizing that the breath of God is breathing right next to and through you.

When you're ready, read this account of a time Jesus was a step ahead of the disciples.

The scene: Jesus had died; the disciples had returned to fishing and hadn't caught anything all night.

> When the sun came up, Jesus was standing on the beach, but they didn't recognize him. Jesus spoke to them: "Good morning! Did you catch anything for breakfast?" They answered, "No." He said, "Throw the net off the right side of the boat and see what happens." They did what he said. All of a sudden there were so many fish in it, they weren't strong enough to pull it in. Then the disciple Jesus loved said to Peter, "It's the Master!" When Simon Peter realized that it was the Master, he threw on some clothes, for he was stripped for work, and dove into the sea. The other disciples came in by boat for they weren't far from land, a hundred yards or so, pulling along the net full of fish. When they got out of the boat, they saw a fire laid, with fish and bread cooking on it. Jesus said, "Bring some of the fish you've just caught." Simon Peter joined them and pulled the net to shore—153 big fish! And even with all those fish, the net didn't rip. Jesus said, "Breakfast is ready." Not one of the disciples dared ask, "Who are you?" They knew it was the Master. (John 21:4–12 MSG)

In your imagination enter the scene as it is pictured in the John account. Feel the rocking of your boat, smell the smells. Jesus has died. It's been a long, unproductive night. How are you feeling as you fish, catching nothing? Close your eyes and feel your emotions as one of the disciples.

You look up and see a small fire on the shore. You see a figure sitting by the fire.[18] It's Jesus! What happens within you (you are one of the disciples) as you see him?

_____

He tells you to throw out your net again. It's immediately filled with squirming fish. Catching them seems somehow effortless.

You come to shore. Smell the fire and the aroma of fish cooking. Look into Jesus's eyes—what do you feel and sense as his eyes meet yours?

_____

Gaze at the picture above. What invitation does it hold for you today? Take time with this. . . .

_____

To close this time with the Lord, listen to song #13 in the "*Savor, the Book*" playlist.

14

MARRIAGE

Continuing the story, the Shulamite has just thrown herself into the king's embrace for the first time. And his joy explodes. How does he show it, being one step ahead?

Song of Songs 3:6–7 (TPT):

> Who is this one ascending from the wilderness in the pillar of the glory cloud? He is fragrant with the anointing oils of myrrh and frankincense—more fragrant than all the spices of the merchant. Look! It is the king's marriage carriage—the love seat surrounded by sixty champions, the mightiest of Israel's host, are like pillars of protection.

He's thinking *marriage*.

Consider the wedding/relationship theme throughout Scripture. Isaiah 54:5–6: "Your [creator] will be your husband." Or Isaiah 62:5: "As the bridegroom rejoices over the bride, so shall your God rejoice over you." The Garden of Pleasure in Genesis, and the couple God made to live there and enjoy the pleasure, have already been mentioned. Then there's the great wedding supper of the Lamb that's coming for all of us who have our oil ready (Revelation 19:9). Jesus is called "Beloved" by his Father after his baptism. And this is just a cursory look at the marriage/ love paradigm.

Oneness . . . Perfect Union

This relationship is not just a marriage but a *union* . . . oneness. Note Jesus's prayers for oneness with his people in John 17. John 17:21: "That they may all be one, **just as you, Father, are in me, and I in you, that they also may be in us,** so that the world may believe that you have sent me." His words seem to tumble over one another as he repeats himself again two verses later in John 17:23: **"I in them and you in me,** that they may **become perfectly one,** so that the world may know that you sent me and loved them even as you loved me."

He's serious about this oneness between us, himself, and the Father. Imagine when his prayer will be answered: complete and joyful *unity* between all people in his kingdom! His prayer that "the world may know" will be fulfilled.

But what might he practically be praying for? Some ethereal, spiritual identity with him in which we will completely share his very being? No doubt something like that.

Human marriage is a picture of the relationship of Christ and the church; Paul tells us that. Consider a healthy human marriage, complete with good, respectful patterns of communication, trust, mutual sharing, serving one another, flirting, joking, enjoying all aspects of this person, including deeply satisfying sex. Is this not a prototype of what Jesus was praying for? I don't know about the physical sex part, but surely this "oneness" includes some pretty amazing, take-your-breath-away times with Jesus, the bridegroom, and us, his bride.

John Burke in *Imagine Heaven* recounts one woman's story of a near-death experience (NDE) and the oneness with Christ she felt in heaven: "Being with him in heaven made me one with him in a way I could never have imagined. I thought what he thought, I dreamed what he dreamed, I felt what he felt."[19]

Another NDEer explained it this way: "This will be hard for people on earth to understand, but I was instantly in Messiah, in him. . . . I knew I was me, and yet I was in Messiah. . . . His love is in a different dimension than our idea of love. There is no question of his love . . . we are in him and he is in us. Yet we don't lose our identity."[20]

The Carriage

Refer back to verses 6–7. This is the king's first mention of marriage (becoming one) in the Song of Solomon. The descriptions of the marriage carriage are beautiful:

- It's comfortable.

- It's colorful with craftsmanship provided by a community of others.

- The fragrance of the gospel—myrrh and frankincense—emanate from the king, reminding us again that he's fully paid for this marriage of oneness with us.

- It's well protected; sixty warriors ("champions") surround it.

Why the need for sixty warriors? One implication might be that marriage/oneness with God is far from easy on this earth. We assume that abiding in Jesus and his peace means a continual lying in the green pastures of Psalm 23. At times it may be peaceful, but the bulk of abiding involves battle: struggles with our old nature, the world, and the enemy. The sixty warriors imply a need for protection and outside help for the couple as they head toward marriage.

Marriage Comes as Trust Grows

As the king puts his wedding dream into place, "his heart full, bursting with joy" (Song of Solomon 3:11 MSG), it's as if he's thinking, *"Okay, I can trust this woman now; she's opening herself completely to me. With the perfect love and security I have for her, we can together go to the hard places of surrender and healing that will complete our oneness. I trust her and can trust my innermost self to her; she's trusting me with her innermost self now too. I can wholeheartedly ask her to marry me. I can't wait for the fulfillment of our oneness, Father!"*

The chapter ends with the joy of the king as he contemplates sitting in this marriage chair with his bride and heading to their wedding. Can you sense the excitement and joy of Christ as he contemplates spiritual oneness with *you*? How do you experience the idea of oneness with him?

Selah

Deep breaths. Be aware of the chair or floor beneath you, holding you up. Think of the chair as a marriage chair you are sharing with the Lord. Or if that idea doesn't sit well with you, think of the chair as the arms of the Father, holding and supporting every part of your body. Feel the solidness of his arms. Relax into him. Smell the fragrance of the gospel. Realize the community of faith that surrounds you, having brought you to this place of growing oneness with Christ.

Now be aware of your body: is there any tension anywhere? Breathe into those places. What's stirring in your soul as you read this?

_____

_____

Listen to song #14 in the "*Savor, the Book*" playlist, closing your eyes and entering the truth that's being sung.

What do you feel inside as you consider this kind of heady, passionate love and companionship from Jesus toward you? Honestly open yourself and all you're experiencing right now, to him. Write down what you're experiencing.

_____

_____

_____

_____

_____

What changes within you as you *know* that this king is now pursuing you, wanting intimacy with you? Write to Christ, telling him how you'd like the intimacy you now enjoy with him to deepen. What would it look like? Feel like? How would you like it to change?

_____

_____

_____

_____

_____

Now allow the Spirit to write you back:

My loved one, my friend . . .

_____

_____

_____

_____

_____

_____

15

MUTUAL PRAISE

SONG OF SOLOMON 4 BRINGS US INTO THE NEAR-BLINDING LIGHT OF THE KING'S ADMIRATION EXPRESSED VERBALLY. The prospect of marriage—oneness, abiding—with the Shulamite brings gushing words from deep wells of the king's own delight and desire.

> Listen, my dearest darling, you are so beautiful—you are beauty itself to me!
> Your eyes are like gentle doves behind your veil.
> What devotion I see each time I gaze upon you.
> You are like a sacrifice ready to be offered.
> When I look at you, I see how you have taken my fruit and tasted my word.
> Your life has become clean and pure, like a lamb washed and newly shorn.
> You now show grace and balance with truth on display.
> Your lips are as lovely as Rahab's scarlet ribbon, speaking mercy, speaking grace.
> The words of your mouth are as refreshing as an oasis.
> What pleasure you bring to me! I see your blushing cheeks
> opened like the halves of a pomegranate,
> showing through your veil of tender meekness.
> When I look at you, I see your inner strength, so stately and strong.
> You are as secure as David's fortress.
> Your virtues and grace cause a thousand famous soldiers to surrender to your beauty.
> Your pure faith and love rest over your heart
> as you nurture those who are yet infants. (4:1–5 TPT)

Songs Jesus Sings Back to Us

Our King Jesus will at times turn the tables on our praises to him and begin to praise us back. Have you ever experienced this? Charles Spurgeon wrote about this. (I have slightly paraphrased his words and removed his original "thee" and "thou" pronouns to aid our reading.)

> To hear Christ turn round upon his Church and seem to say to her: "You have praised me, I will praise you; you think much of me, I think quite as much of you; you use great expressions to me, I will use just the same to you. You say my love is better than wine, so is yours to me; you say my word is sweeter than honey to your lips, the words from your lips are like honey to me. All that you say of me, I say to you. I can see my own beauty in you. Whatever belongs to me, belongs to you. Therefore, O my love, I will sing back the song that you have sung to me." [21]

Have you ever experienced the Lord gently silencing your singing of a worship song to him in order for him to sing the words back to you? We hear the song with a whole new meaning! In one way this experience can make us feel about one inch tall, but in another, we are elevated into the clean and bracing air of his lavish opinion of us. He rejoices over us with singing (Zephaniah 3:17). The next time you hear him singing over and to you, record the words of his song and luxuriate in the messages.

Selah

Settle back and breathe deeply for a bit. Quiet your inner self.

How do you react to the idea of the Lord God singing praise to you? Have you ever sensed him doing this to you?

_____

_____

Take a moment and consider your usual self-talk to and about yourself. What are your typical themes? What adjectives or descriptors do you use concerning yourself? Contrast this with how the Lord is speaking to you.

_____

_____

Deep breaths again. Settle your mind. Then read the passage at the beginning of this chapter one more time.

What words or phrases stand out? Remember that our Lord doesn't see us with fallen human eyes. He sees us as our spirit-self: pure, white, stately, and glorious with his glory.

_____

_____

Do any of the phrases make you shrink in shame? Or cause eye-rolling? These are phrases he wants to sift and purify. Bring them to him.

_____

_____

What phrase or words do you long for him to sing to you from the passage? or other words?

_____

_____

If you want to, ask him now to sing his personal song to you. Hear it with your spirit-ears. Remember the key phrases.

Listen to song #15 in the "*Savor, the Book*" playlist; note the words the Lord sings to you.

16

INVITATION TO TRUST

BASKING IN THE KING'S PRAISE RELEASES CONFIDENCE IN THE SHULAMITE. His words about what he sees in her seem to float above her head, causing her to rise up to become what he says. She makes some decisions.

Song of Songs 4:6 (TPT):

> I've made up my mind. Until the darkness disappears and the dawn has fully come, in spite of shadows and fears, I will go to the mountaintop with you—the mountain of suffering love and the hill of burning incense. Yes, I will be your bride.

She speaks with a bit of trepidation; she realizes entering marriage with him will involve her own suffering (the original language is the "mountain of myrrh"). She acknowledges her fear while bravely stepping into the king's invitation to oneness.

Realizing her caution and the amount of trust the Shulamite is expressing in him, the king speaks: "Now you are ready, my bride, to come with me as we climb the highest peaks together. Come with me through the archway of trust. We will look down from the crest of the glistening mounts and from the summit of our sublime sanctuary, from the lion's den and the leopard's lair" (Song of Solomon 4:8 TPT).

His invitation is to come *with him* through the archway of trust. Stepping through this archway is like stepping from a realm of fear (the lion's den and leopard's lair) into a high place involving trust (the highest peaks.) The king knows what's ahead for her—another dark night—this one much more difficult. He prepares her by focusing her on the necessity of trusting him.

What might the Shulamite be fearing at this point? Perhaps fears for her relationship with this wild man who gallops over mountains. Anxiety about what her family or others will think. Marriage itself? Will the couple be pleased with each other?

She also may fear what this "mountain of myrrh" is all about.

Selah

Take some deep breaths. Reorient your awareness to the trustworthiness of the God who is surrounding you and breathing within you. Relax into this place of safety and security.

Look at the picture[22] above.

Is there an area of life or a situation in which you need to walk through an archway of trust with the Lord, something he's asking you to trust him with or for? Ask him.

_____

_____

What's beyond this archway of trust for you? What concerns do you have if you walk through it?

_____

_____

What would it be like to be on the other side of the arch, fully trusting?

_____

_____

If it's meaningful to you, imagine walking with the Lord through the arch in this scene. What do you need from him in order to go to the other side? How do you experience Jesus going through it with you?

_____

_____

_____

Now listen to song #16 in the "*Savor,* the Book" playlist, taking in the words of trust, feeling their meaning.

17

WINDS OF ADVERSITY

SONG OF SOLOMON 4:16 (TPT):

> Awake, O north wind! Awake, O south wind! Breathe on my garden with
> your Spirit-Wind. Stir up the sweet spice of your life within me. Spare
> nothing as you make me your fruitful garden. Hold nothing back until I
> release your fragrance. Come walk with me as you walked with Adam in
> your paradise garden. Come taste the fruits of your life in me.

The words of love, pleasure, and delight from the king in chapter 4 cause the
Shulamite to long to provide a place for him to come and enjoy her life. A desire to
minister to *him* begins to form. She thirsts to delight him with her companionship,
and she calls upon the north and south winds to create places within her that are
worthy of him.

North and south winds denote strong weather—storms, cold, and heat. She calls
upon (without naming) adversity and perhaps pain in order that she may release
his fragrance and become his equal in oneness.

****

Jesus: *I want to tell you a story.*

Me: *Okay! (I settle in)*

Jesus: *Once upon a time there was a woman who made and cared for small pots.
These were the kind of pots that people plant things in. Also, they were very decorative.*

Each day the woman watched carefully over the formation of the pots, making sure they were strong and well made.

One day as she was working in her outdoor studio, a vicious storm arose. Quickly she tried to cover the pots with tarps. The wind howled, whipping up stinging rain and driving branches and leaves across the space. She realized the storm was becoming dangerous, so she took cover in her house. With worry she watched the tumultuous weather work its fury on her many pots, wondering how they were faring.

At long last the storm abated, and she hurried out to survey the damage. The pots were filled with water, and she noticed one or two were cracked. Only one pot, though, was truly broken, lying in pieces.

The woman realized with wonder that her pots were actually really good at holding water as well as a host of other things that came into them from the storm. She lovingly took the broken and cracked pot and fixed it, using metal and glue. The broken container with the cracks actually became the one people liked the most.

Jesus: *What do you think is the point of this story?*

Me: *I'm thinking of the people I care about and love. There's some painful stuff going on in their lives. You are saying the winds and rain in their lives, or in my life too, aren't all bad. Storms of life actually prove their (and my) worth and purpose?*

Jesus: *Yes, and the pot the woman repaired was actually stronger and more beautiful because of the storm. Allow the storms of life to further prove your purpose and worth. And remember that I, the Master Potter, am the one to repair the damage that's sure to come because of storms. Don't fear storms, Val—yours or anyone else's. They're actually your friends.*

The Supreme Worth of a Struggle

A trusting, surrendered heart is what helps us go through times of pain and struggle. All of us have experienced times of suffering: the death of someone close to us or the death of a vision. A setback, career-wise or financially. Health issues appear out of the blue. It's really hard to trust especially when the dark time seems to go on and on. The Shulamite is about to experience such a time, perhaps precipitated by her very calling of the winds to blow upon her life.

In a time of deep emotional pain and struggle some years ago, I asked the Lord (with anger) why all this was happening to me. He quietly said, "I'm just answering your prayer." He immediately brought to mind my prayer as a new believer: that I would know him as deeply and as well as a human could. *So—all this crap I'm going through, and feeling, is* my *fault?*

Jesus always has purpose for the storms of life. He may just be answering our prayers. Storms prove our purpose; we discover gifts and strengths we didn't know we had. We experience a depth of relating with him that we couldn't have attained otherwise. Job's storm brought him face to face with what he was afraid of, and he had to walk *through* that fear with God (Job 3:25).

Sometimes a storm comes simply as a test—tests have to do with spiritual advancement in ministry and authority, and Jesus always wants us to pass. We know storms are good, both cognitively and from experience. But that doesn't mean they aren't excruciating.

A Butterfly

I like to picture this struggle with the storms of life metaphorically as a caterpillar turning into a butterfly:

Caterpillar: the larva of a butterfly, of the earth, creeping slowly along.

The chrysalis: the stage of transformation that takes time and comes at a cost.

Cocoon: the casing of protection around the butterfly as it transforms. The cocoon is broken off only with violence.

Butterfly: our spirit-self and new nature Jesus has already given us, constantly supernaturally forming.

The cost of transformation for a butterfly involves some difficult steps. One is that its "skin" must be shed several times in the process because the skin becomes too small for its changing body. There is a struggle to burst out of what once fit but no longer does. Next, the emerging butterfly must beat its wings hard and repeatedly against the walls of the cocoon so the wings will form properly. If a well-meaning human comes along, sees the tiny beating wings inside a cocoon, and helpfully wants to aid the butterfly by opening the cocoon prematurely, that butterfly will die.

Months, years of beating my wings against seeming obstacles? I identify with this.

Selah

Take some deep breaths. Invite the Holy Spirit's input as you reflect.

When you go through a time of struggle, either materially, emotionally, or spiritually, what's your typical reaction?

_____

_____

How does this response work for you?

_____

_____

Read "Welcoming Prayer,"[23] by Mary Mrozowski:

Welcome, welcome, welcome.
I welcome everything that comes to me today because I know it's for my healing.
I welcome all thoughts, feelings, emotions, persons, situations, and conditions.
I let go of my desire for power and control.
I let go of my desire for affection, esteem, approval, and pleasure.
I let go of my desire for survival and security.
I let go of my desire to change any situation, condition, person, or myself.
I open to the love and presence of God and God's action within. Amen.

How do you react to this prayer?

_____

_____

For me, praying this prayer slowly, honestly, and several times a day when I'm undergoing a dark time helps keep me centered on Jesus. The prayer does *not* encourage us to welcome abuse, death, or pain itself; rather, it enables us not to get knocked off our perch of being *above* the struggle (Colossians 3:1) as we trust him to work everything out for our good. The prayer prods our eyes back to God as we let go of the things mentioned.

Is there any "strong wind" situation in your life now that you need to surrender, honestly praying this prayer? If so, spend some time praying through each line of the Welcoming Prayer, listening for the Lord's response in words, pictures, or senses.

_____

_____

_____

Consider how the word translated as *spirit* in Greek is *pneuma,* which means "breath" or "wind." Listen to song #17 in the "*Savor,* the Book" playlist, realizing that the winds of life can be infused with the spirit of life. If it resonates, pray this song back to the Lord.

Ask Jesus to show you his emotional response to you when you're in a storm of life. Record any impressions, pictures, or words from him.

_____

_____

18

SECOND DARK NIGHT

THE SHULAMITE IS ABOUT TO HIT NEW DEPTHS IN HER ONENESS WITH THE KING.

Setting the scene: she and the king have been enjoying intimacy in the garden (Song of Solomon 5:1). She's recently called upon the winds of adversity to blow upon her life, making her fit for her king. (*Uh-oh . . .*)

Then the king comes knocking in verse 2.

> I heard my lover knocking and calling: "Open to me, my treasure, my darling, my dove, my perfect one. My head is drenched with dew, my hair with the dampness of the night." But I responded, "I have taken off my robe. Should I get dressed again? I have washed my feet. Should I get them soiled?" (Song of Solomon 5:2–3 NLT)

Why does he have to knock when they've been together in the garden? He knocks because she's hiding behind a wall with a locked door (2:9 and 5:5–6). There are belief systems, areas of self-rule, walled-off areas within her that bar him entrance into her inner self. These walls prevent her from becoming the confident, stunning person of beauty and honor whom he's making her to be, and it's time to do the hard work of emancipation. The butterfly's wings are beginning to beat against the cocoon.

Clues into her mindset come from her response to his call. Verse 3 paraphrased: "Why do I need to come out from behind this wall? After all, I've let you cleanse me—you helped me take off my filthy clothes of sin, forgave me, and gave me entrance to heaven with these new robes of righteousness. **Isn't that enough?"**

The king gives a resounding no in answer to this last question; he's not content to have a puppet for a wife. His hair is "damp with dew"—reminiscent of the Garden of Gethsemane. His sacrifice at the cross has bought far more than just a get-out-of-hell-free card. He wants intimacy, relationship with no walls. He desires untamed freedom within the wideness and brightness of all their union can bring. He wants a bride who is equal to him, able to rule and reign with him. She's nowhere near that yet with this tepid response.

His request to open to him is an invitation to get out of her cocoon. It is time to for the Shulamite to come out from behind the wall.

Walls and Locks

Walls in the Song of Songs represent areas of pseudo-safety within us . . . places behind which we hide. The problem is that we don't usually realize we have walls or that we are hiding behind them. Early-childhood trauma can leave us with *implicit memories*, memories that can't be consciously recalled but nevertheless affect behavior in the present. We also have *semantic memory*, things we remember, plus narratives we've told ourselves that helped make sense of our childhood stories.

We all have many neural pathways in our brains, made up of both positive and fearful memories. Pathways surrounding particularly traumatic events are hard to access, but the Lord sees them and in his perfect timing wants to bring them to the light and heal them. Dark nights shake loose the iron grip of our self-protection, bring about eventual surrender to his power and love, and in the process re-form neural pathways into health.

Some common "walls":

- Strategies we employ to protect ourselves from feeling fear or shame
- Refusing to accept the forgiveness, cleansing, and new self of the cross

- Robotically doing what others expect or demand with no consideration of personal needs or desires

- Habits we are afraid to admit to or afraid for others to see

- Challenging and/or intimidation of or from others

- Vows meant to protect and narratives we believe that have little or no basis in reality

Locks represent our self-talk and justifications for being behind the wall:

- "My anxiety (fear) isn't a big deal; I live fine with it, okay?"

- "I'm just not the kind of person who opens up; I'm private."

- "There's no way I'm gonna let people know I struggle with *that*."

- "I'm never trying that again—no way."

- "It's never worked before . . . so I'm giving up."

Clues that there may be a wall we're hiding behind:

- Inappropriate or out-of-proportion responses or behaviors

- Convoluted strategies to avoid certain people or circumstances

- A memory or personal issue that we know the Lord wants us to address—but we just don't

Pause here and consider these walls, locks, and clues. Which are ones you recognize in yourself?

We stay locked up within our self-ruling, self-protecting kingdom, not realizing that the very God we're praying to for help is now inviting us to emerge and, with him, deal with this baggage. He wants us to release to him our convoluted efforts to protect ourselves, to vomit out all the struggle, anger, and pain, to let go of our many ropes, hit bottom, and surrender everything to him. Any serious desire for intimacy with Jesus includes addressing walls and locks, hard though it may be.

"Un-answers" to Prayer

Going more deeply, walls can also be situations in life in which God is not seeming to answer prayer. We ask him for healing, provision of finances, help for a struggling marriage, or for wayward loved ones to return to Christ. Indeed, God can seem like a brick wall when our prayers bounce back to us seemingly unheard. We search out Bible promises; we pray them sometimes for years, seemingly to no avail. Things in our life aren't lining up with what the Bible teaches, and over time we can get weary, mad, or depressed. Some of us silence our doubt, quote verses, and tough it out. Our thoughts can gradually slide into an unbelief that he even cares.

It can feel as though we're fighting Satan. We rebuke, resist, plead the blood of Christ. We go through spiritual or mental gymnastics trying to get on top of these issues. We study the Bible and read books that purport to have the answer. Some of us hit a local pub, porn site, or turn to substances to make it through these times. We can wear ourselves out trying to get a prayer answered or to maneuver ourselves into a place where *this issue* goes away.

What's Really Going On Here?

To completely understand the Lord's way or to unequivocally answer the "why" of our particular struggle is impossible. His ways are above ours. However, we know that he sees areas deep in our souls that desperately need his love. He sees the kingdom of self-rule inside us—sees it in living color—and we don't even know that kingdom exists. He sees trauma in early life that affects our neural pathways, pain that results in our knee-jerk, iron-clad self-protection.

Each wall he brings to light is custom designed by him to affect those deep neural pathways and to bring transformation into our very brain chemicals as we come out from behind that wall. Paradoxically, his seeming withdrawal, leaving us to the ravages of pain and struggle, is the precise recipe to most thoroughly bring healing and relief. Why? Because we come to the end of our many ropes. We hit bottom and finally—finally—allow love to conquer us. It's a delicious way to lose a war—truly.

Particularly in the case of unanswered prayer over years, deepening intimacy can sometimes require the Lord to smash the hold that Scripture has on our mind and belief system. "You search the Scriptures because you think they give you eternal life. But the Scriptures point to me," Jesus states in John 5:39 (NLT). The truth is, we walk with a person, not a book.

Trust

Trust defined: *Firm belief in the reliability, truth, ability, or strength of someone.*[24]

Look at the picture[25] above as you consider the definition of trust. What stirs within your body and emotions as you place yourself in this scene, becoming the person on the ladder trusting Christ? Focusing on the picture's perspective, what is important for your own safety?

_____

The above picture represents an area of life for which you need to trust God or an area you need to trust him with. What fears come up? Write these feelings or doubts to him:

_____

_____

A deeper surrender to the person of Christ means choosing trust that cannonballs us over a seeming void—*"Are you really there, Lord? What if this ladder breaks?"*—and we discover his love tightly gripping us. Choosing to *fight* to trust him opens the door to freshness and to a closer intimacy with Jesus and with ourselves that seems almost unfathomable. With this new trust, neural pathways begin to relax, change, and grow, yielding confidence and peace.

We lean into these dark nights; they're our friends.

Fruit of Trust

During dark nights, our relationship with Christ shifts from "what verse applies where" to joy and freedom in a garden of pleasure. Over time the issue (health, the wayward child, marriage, unanswered prayer) ceases to become the issue, and our relationship with Jesus becomes central. Our Lord has a deeper objective than just answering our prayer. He could do that, of course—just answer and give us what we want—but he won't leave the "kingdom of self" intact.

Selah

It's time for some leaning into the spirit of wisdom. Relax. Get into a comfortable position and quiet your body and mind by breathing deeply. Allow your mind to roam through memories of the Lord's trustworthiness to you in the past. Were some of those times born from times of suffering?

Listen to song #18 in the "*Savor, the Book*" playlist in preparation for the questions below.

When you're ready, review the list of "walls," "locks," and "clues" above.

Look at the picture[26] below. Imagine standing behind this wall, looking out at the scene beyond. What do you feel? What stands out to you from this picture?

_____

_____

Ask the Lord, "Jesus, is there a wall in my life I'm standing behind? If I am, what descriptor word do you put on the wall, Lord? Describe this wall to me." (Wait on his word—along with a word you'd put on it.)

_____

_____

What's my self-talk surrounding this wall?

_____

_____

If I open the gate and come out from behind this wall, what's ahead for me?

_____

_____

What action is needed for me to get beyond this wall?

_____

_____

Is there a prayer that has remained unanswered for some time? If so, what has the Lord said to you about it, or what is he saying now?

_____

_____

_____

19

THE FIGHT

Back to the narrative—the Shulamite gets up and unlocks the door, hands dripping with myrrh. Myrrh = embalming spice (used when something or someone dies).

Song of Solomon 5:5–6:

> I arose to open to my beloved, and my hands dripped with myrrh, my fingers with liquid myrrh, on the handles of the bolt. I opened to my beloved, but my beloved had turned and gone. My soul failed me when he spoke. I sought him, but found him not; I called him, but he gave no answer.

She turns the handle, gets out from behind her wall . . . but he's gone. His silence rings hollow in the night. She now has a choice: get mad at his vanishing act or press forward, trusting his love, going where she last heard his voice calling her.

Twice above she calls him her "beloved." She reminds herself of his cherishing love. Choosing trust over anger, she puts her hand to the lock.

Notice how love itself gets her out from behind her walls of fear, shame, and stiff-arming. Willpower alone won't do it, and willpower certainly won't last. Memories of sweetness, eating love apples, laughing with her beloved, recalling his words of affirmation, enjoying the banner of "love" over her head: all of these enable the rough work of entering places she doesn't want to go, of forsaking old patterns. Lasting change comes when we seek a living Christ rather than simply a solution to our issues.

The Keepers of the Wall

The Shulamite enters the city—where she had found her beloved before. But this time he isn't in the city. She searches, really wanting him now. Song of Solomon 5:7: "The watchmen found me as they went about in the city; they beat me, they bruised me, they took away my veil, those watchmen of the walls."

Her second dark night is quite a bit worse than her first. When she sought her beloved in the city the first time, she encountered the grace of the gospel, finding her king fairly quickly. This time she is beat up by the watchmen, or overseers. Overseers in Hebrew: "*the keepers of the wall; those who **make the rounds.**"

These keepers of the wall represent—

- Our thinking processes that go round and round, surrounding hurt, anger, or painful experiences.

- Narratives we rehearse over and over to ourselves that result in wrong conclusions and misbeliefs.

The Shulamite has a mighty fight with these overseers—she's bruised, beaten, and wounded—and in the process, her veil is removed.

Veils

Examples of veils:

- Beliefs, dearly held convictions, political opinions, narratives of past experiences that we rehash over and over

- Memories or mental strategies that keep God at arm's length

- False beliefs about God, others, or us, things we've perhaps been taught by well-meaning but incorrect mentors

- Suppressed secrets or negative feelings we're "not supposed to have"

- Lost dreams or hopes

- Mindsets that keep us cowering in fear and shame

Similar to the skins of a transforming butterfly, veils are ripped off in the course of beating our wings against the cocoon wall. Attempts to cognitively grasp what exactly my particular veil or wall is—so that I can control or fix it—only prolongs the process. The fight transcends mental understanding. This is like blind hand-to-hand combat, not knowing where we are going but continuing with the assurance of relief if we just *stay. in. the. fight.*

The Shulamite at last stumbles out into her morning, imploring the witnesses to help her. Song of Solomon 5:8: "I adjure you, O daughters of Jerusalem, if you find my beloved, that you tell him I am sick with love."

She's exhausted from the fight, veil-less, broken. She has nothing left but a naked desire for her king. Abiding in his love, eyes and lips locked with his, has replaced desire for anything else. She is peacefully surrendered. Even the legitimate question of why he suddenly disappeared right when she decided to open the door to him fades into a quiet sense of just wanting him, him alone.

She desires him, with his embrace and warmth. The dark night of the soul is doing its work; her soul and senses are being purified deeply where her will and self-control can't penetrate. Peace replaces shame and fear; strategies of self-protection lie broken under her feet.

Dark Nights—Unique to Our History

Any dark night a human enters will take shape around the particular core lies/beliefs and narratives of that human's past memories and experience. The Shulamite's dark night involved walls of shame and fear; she felt dark and preferred to be content simply hiding in a protected space. She was okay just with salvation. Her wall protected her from having to come out where others could see her in her imagined ugliness—actually her great beauty. Although she understood the gospel in her head, it took a terrific fight for this knowledge to sink completely down into her "knowing." It took bruising and wounding to unchain her from her "old nature" mindset.

A dark night typically occurs when Jesus is getting ready to reveal to us who we are in him, in detail and uniqueness. It comes as a prelude to the unveiling of our promise and what he really means by that promise. An emerging butterfly—strong from the fight to exit the cocoon—is just on the cusp.

A Personal Dark Night

My main dark night went on for about ten years. When I was eighteen years old, God gave me a life promise, and from that point on I had notions about how my life was going to look. My fight to bring this promise to pass was intermittent during my "dark night" years but gradually deepened in intensity as I fought God. I tried in every way I could think of to get my vision of his will to unfold. I believed I had the right verses. I had biblical principles to prove this was his will for me.

Oh, the anger when nothing "worked"! I was surrendered to him on the outside, but inside I was full of turmoil. To shorten a long story, I eventually threw my vision of the promise at him and stated that I was giving up. No more would I try to follow his will because—"it doesn't work, God. I'm *done.*" I felt tired, resigned, still mad at him for not doing his part, but with a smidgen of peace.

Many months went on. I was introduced to prayer exercises that enabled me to connect with him. A quiet submission—a desire for his true will—began to bloom within. I still felt that I'd somehow missed something he wanted for me, but it felt good not to be fighting anymore.

More months passed during which his face became more central to my vision. *Oh!* His love was beginning to delight me. New abilities to hear him—through inner pictures, words, song lyrics, sensations in my body—grew, and the inner conversations with him smoothed into more of a continual spirit-to-Spirit communion. This Man. This Jesus is what I want. Over time I saw his promises being fulfilled, but with such rest on my part.

You see, my walls were in the realm of worthlessness and inadequacy. I head-believed the opposite about myself of course: *"I'm strong in the strength of his might!"* But inside the dark recess of my brain, a little Val was cowering in the corner (behind a wall), terrified of discovering that I really was worthless. My ten-year fight began to end as Jesus gently approached little me, took me in his arms, and healed memories both semantic and implicit (ones I remembered and ones I wasn't conscious of). I'd never want to repeat the struggle of those years, but I'm eternally glad I went through the experience!

Selah

When you're ready, become quiet in Jesus's presence. As always, get comfortable and begin to breathe deeply. Anticipate his quiet leadership as you reflect on your personal fight.

Listen to song #19 in the "*Savor,* the Book" playlist. This song beautifully expresses the Lord's presence with us in tough times and his purposes that eclipse the struggle.

Talk (or write) about any fight you're sensing within yourself. This might present as inner turmoil or a place of unrest. Describe the struggle.

_____

_____

Is there something you need to die to, an area of "myrrh"?

_____

_____

What are the "keepers of the wall, those who make the rounds" in your mind?

_____

_____

Ask Jesus to rephrase in his words what he'd like the keepers of your wall—your narratives and self-talk—to sound and look like:

_____

_____

Do you sense that there's a veil clouding your vision? If so, what is it? (You can refer to the examples of possible veils above if that helps.)

_____

_____

Look at the picture[27] below. How does a veil obscure what you see?

What veils have clouded your picture of **Christ** in your life?

_____

_____

If it resonates, imagine this veil being removed by Jesus himself. He pulls it away from your face, lifts it off your head and shoulders, and drops it to the ground. You can now see his face clearly. What do his eyes and face convey to you?

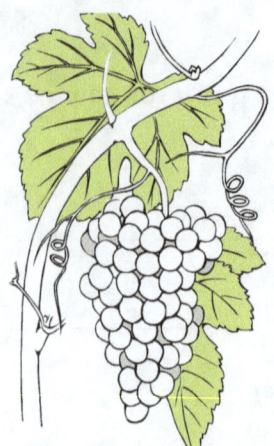

20

THE FACE OF GOD

JACOB (HIS NAME MEANS "THE SUPPLANTER, ONE WHO CIRCUMVENTS") EXPERIENCED A DARK NIGHT, AS SEEN IN GENESIS 32. He fights with a "Man," mirroring the fight the Shulamite experienced in her dark night. Jacob's story helps flesh out what's going on in these times.

As you remember, Jacob was the younger son of Isaac and Rebecca, younger than his twin, Esau, by a few minutes. God had given promises to Rebecca concerning Jacob in Genesis 25: "The elder will serve the younger," thus giving Jacob firstborn inheritance rights. At the time of Jacob's fight with God, he is being called out from behind a wall of fear—fear that he's carried for about twenty years.

Back then he and his mom had cheated Esau out of his firstborn rights, as well as the firstborn blessing. Esau had responded to this manipulation and deception as you'd suppose: he vowed to kill Jacob. Jacob then fled to his Uncle Laban, sharpening his own human skills of bargaining, manipulating, and deceiving, resulting in great wealth.

As time goes on, his uncle becomes angry at Jacob's actions and jealous of the obvious blessing of God on Jacob's life. Things heat up relationally between them. God tells Jacob to leave: "Return to the land of your fathers *and to your kindred* [specifically Esau, the one who wants him dead], and I will be with you" (Genesis 31:3, emphasis added).

We pick up the story in Genesis 32. Jacob obeys God, taking his flocks, herds, and large family back toward his family of origin. On his way, "the angels of God met him" (Genesis 32:1). Seeing these heavenly beings, Jacob declares triumphantly, "Mahanaim! This is God's camp!" (see 32:2). *Mahanaim* means two camps; that is, a camp of God and his own earthly camp. Bolstered with this evidence of God's angelic favor toward him, he sends messengers ahead to meet Esau. The report comes back: Esau is on his way to meet Jacob—with a group of four hundred men.

Jacob, the man who had received a clear command from God to return home, including a sure promise of God's presence with him the entire time, and with an angel escort no less, crumbles into panic. He decides to divide his household into two camps (Mahanaim) in his human effort to protect his family. He reasons that at least one camp will make it out alive after Esau's reception.

In his panic he turns to God in prayer—this shows his true heart condition below all the conniving and deception. He humbles himself. He honestly expresses his fear and ends his prayer with a reminder of God's promise to protect and enlarge him. He takes his wives and children across the Jabbok River (*Jabbok* means "emptying or containing nothing") and returns to the east side. He's about to face an emptying that even he can't manipulate or circumvent.

Jacob's Dark Night

During Jacob's dark night, he finds himself alone; a Man wrestles with him through the night. The phrasing is significant: "A man wrestled with *him*" (Genesis 32:24, emphasis added). This man, according to Bible scholars, is an Old Testament appearance of the second person of the Trinity, Jesus. Jesus initiates this fight and toward morning wounds his son Jacob in the hip. The hip wound weakens Jacob, but he still won't surrender: "I will not let you go unless you bless me" (32:26). The prolonged wrestling brings out Jacob's deep desire: to be blessed by God—for God's promise that "the older will serve the younger" to be answered. He had tried everything in his (and his mother's) power to get that promise humanly fulfilled but now cowers in fear of his life from the one—Esau—who stands in his way. He is being stripped of all human dodging and bravado.

Jesus bruises Jacob's hip. Dark nights involve pain and sometimes loss. Jesus, seeing that Jacob's desire for blessing is becoming purified, asks, "What is your name?" "Jacob," he answers (32:27). Jesus, of course, knows his name. He wants Jacob to see *himself* and admit who he is apart from Christ: *I am the Supplanter, the Grasper, the Deceiver.* Jacob has to experience and admit his own sinful nature and his impotence to bring the promise of God to pass. He has to die to who he used to be in order for God's purposes for his chosen nation to be birthed.

Following the confession, Jesus changes Jacob's name and his identity to *Israel*—"One who struggled with God and prevailed" (32:29), or possibly "God rules."

Jacob calls this holy place Peniel—"Face of God." He has not only seen but also touched, fought, and submitted to God himself.

In the light of the dawning day, Jacob limps out into his destiny, worn out but feeling weightless: his old, deceptive, manipulative nature a thing of the past. He meets Esau as a new man—one with a new name ringing in his ears, one with a destiny and a part to play in the kingdom of God.

It takes a mighty fight to apprehend our own healing and destiny. Jesus transforms us into people who are able to stand the weight and glory of his calling, through the very struggle of a dark season. Oh, the importance and breadth of meaning for each dark night we enter! These times are not just random happenings in a fallen world.

Selah

As usual, begin by taking some deep breaths to quiet your inner being. Allow you mind to graze on Jacob's story recounted above. What stands out to you from the narrative?

_____

Put yourself in the place of the Shulamite or Jacob, whichever 'fight" story you connect with. Have you experienced this kind of struggle before? Are you in one now?

How does it feel, or has it felt, to be wrestling with Jesus?

_____

Listen to song #20 in the "*Savor,* the Book" playlist before continuing.

Pause before the power that God has to submit us to his perfect will. Reflect on how the love of Jesus has drawn you into painful struggles with him as he seeks to unveil your destiny.

What emotions are you feeling now?

_____

_____

How do you believe God feels as he watches you fight him, or his feelings as he watched your past fights with him?

_____

_____

What are you really wrestling for? Or against?

_____

_____

Ask him what encouragement he has for you now in this season of your life:

_____

_____

In a fight with God and our destiny, walls topple. Locks vanish under death blows to our vision and the control of our lives. We hear the ringing words of Jesus to us: "I love you, and I always will!"

21

THE FINDING

AT THIS POINT THE SHULAMITE IS EXHAUSTED FROM HER FIGHT WITH THE OVERSEERS. She's also faint with love. The witnesses bring focus to her tired mind with two questions.

First Question

"Why is your lover better than all others? What makes your lover so special?" (Song of Solomon 5:9 NLT).

"What is it about him that you love?" In the original language she answers by describing his physical body in detail, signifying her focus on the intimate parts of him that he's given to her. She realizes that this man and his love are truly all she wants. The remembrance of the wall and the fight with the keepers of the wall is fading. She ends chapter 5 with a description of her lover's mouth and his kiss; intimacy with him has become central to her now. She realizes this love truly is the only thing left for her; gifts of people, beauty, ministry, health, answered prayer, and wealth aren't a focus anymore. Just him. His love and companionship. His kiss is just that powerful.

Second Question

"Where has the one who loves you gone? Which way did he turn?" (6:1 NIRV).

She considers this question and discovers what I believe is the apex—the high point—of the book. "My love has gone down to his garden. He's gone to the beds of spices. He's eating in the gardens. I belong to my love, and he belongs to me!" (6:2–3 NIRV).

My paraphrase: "Oh! He's right here! Right here *inside* me and he's not leaving! I *do* belong to him, and he belongs to me—for all time! He and I are *one*. My thoughts = his thoughts. My spirit = one spirit with his!"

Oneness blooms into fullness as she realizes where he is: inside her very self. "*I don't have to go looking outside of myself for him anymore. No more seeking emotional, Holy-Spirit high times to prove he's with me, no more searching for evidence of his love while I secretly fear he doesn't care. No more negativity about myself. He's the Word (a vehicle of communication) living inside me, and furthermore—I now know I'm his and he is mine!*"

Exquisite, cascading feelings of being loved with no walls between the woman and her lover—this is the sublime delight that the king gives—an unbarred, unencumbered relationship where love has no boundaries, a broad, open place of sunlight and joy. The walls blocking this bliss are gone!

Recap:

Jesus, gazing at her with happiness: "I am yours, and you are mine."

The Shulamite, responding with dawning realization: "I am yours. And you are mine!"

Consider what this means. Jesus—God—*belongs* to us. This implies that all his resources—wisdom, love, power, discretion, glory, fun, lightness, along with his sorrow—are ours. We co-own all that is Jesus. Within our chamber of intimacy with him, we think, react, emote, reason—with his mind and spirit commingling with ours.

Do we realize the vast implications for our lives, for the world surrounding us every day? Do we live in the good of this gift of Jesus *belonging* to us? I do not, not constantly anyway.

Immediately upon her realization that he's inside her in fullness (they're "one" in a truly married and abiding way), the king's words tumble out in happiness:

"You're beautiful, like Tirzah! (delight, pleasantness, pleasure)
Actually you're beautiful, like Jerusalem! (a city of peace)
And you're majestic, like an army with banners! Formidable!"
(Song of Solomon 6:4, author's paraphrase)

She has become delight, peace, strength. Having survived the bruising, the heartache of walls, the darkness of unanswered prayer, she emerges now as a force to be reckoned with. Indeed, she's bonded—fused—to him in ways she never could have conjured or thought about prior to her dark night. Her confidence in his love has strengthened considerably; she's on her way to becoming a bride worthy of him.

The king goes on with superlatives to describe to others what she's become. "Who is this woman? She is like the sunrise in all its glory. She is as beautiful as the moon. She is as bright as the sun. She is as majestic as the stars traveling across the sky" (6:10 NIRV).

The love of Jesus and a journey into intimacy have created this creature. She has responded to the king's initiation by resolutely marching out from behind her walls; her cocoon has broken open, and a beautiful butterfly is emerging. This is what our God wants us as individuals to be . . . formidable. As a community of his lovers, we become an offensive force for the kingdom. We are strong under his banner of love. Can we trust that this is the purpose of all the struggles we endure in life? Can we surrender to his purposes?

Selah

Settle yourself and take deep breaths. Allow your awareness to come to your interior center, where Jesus himself abides. Rest in him as you quiet your brain.

What does it practically mean to you that Christ is inside you, in your garden or vineyard? Do you have questions or emotions that surface about this? Write down your reaction.

_____

_____

_____

When you're ready, read the passage as it is unpacked below, taken from Ephesians 3:17–20 (TPT).

Read slowly. Underline the words or phrases that jump out at you:

- The resting place of his love will become the very source and root of your life.

- You will be empowered to discover what every holy one experiences—the great magnitude of the astonishing love of Christ in all its dimensions.

- How deeply intimate and far-reaching is his love! How enduring and inclusive it is!

- Endless love beyond measurement.

- Extravagant love pours into you until you are filled to overflowing with the fullness of God!

- Never doubt God's mighty power to work in you and accomplish all this.

- He will achieve infinitely more than your greatest request, your most unbelievable dream, and exceed your wildest imagination!

Read the words you underlined. What emotions do you experience (looking at the feelings wheel, page 11) as you repeat these words to yourself? How does your body feel?

Is there an invitation from God to you from this passage?

Ask for these phrases to be operational in your life. Listen for a response from Jesus. How is he reacting to your prayer?

Listen to song #21 in the "*Savor, the Book*" playlist. If you'd like, dance around with the Lord as you listen to this rendering of what oneness is all about.

22

SUPERNATURAL BEGINNINGS

THE OLD DARK, SHAME-FILLED, IN-HIDING SHULAMITE HAS TRANSFORMED INTO AN AWESOME ARMY WITH BANNERS. This has been a supernatural work of epic proportions, birthed from the king's lavish love, words, and power, aided by her choice to trust and agree with him.

Some exciting changes are now happening in her behavior.

Song of Solomon 6:11: (She): "I went down to the nut orchard to look at the blossoms of the valley, to see whether the vines had budded, whether the pomegranates were in bloom."

She initiates an outward focus, going forth to look for other gardens that are budding. Her self-centeredness is broadening to include other people and their gardens. She wants to learn from them, share garden secrets with them, aid them where she can in their growth. Community spreads.

A notable change is also happening in how others view her. Song of Solomon 6:13 (ERV):

(Others) "Shulamith! come back, come back, so we may look at you. Why are you staring at Shulamith, as she dances the Mahanaim dance?"

Recall where this word *Mahanaim* comes from. Jacob named his angelic protection squad *Mahanaim*, meaning an angel camp was added to his natural, earthly family camp. Interesting how this same word resurfaces in the Song of Solomon.

The Shulamite has started dancing with angels. No longer is she relying solely on her natural, earthly resources; she's dancing with and using the king's supernatural assets that she now knows are *inside her*, and others are noticing.

Dancing with Angels

The supernatural riches of our king gradually become part of our lives as he begins to trust us with deeper understanding and experiences of his love. If you are like me, you've longed for the power-filled demonstrations that Scripture presents almost matter-of-factly. Waters literally parting, broken limbs immediately made straight. The Song of Solomon indicates that this very thing is in our future and, in fact, our present as we walk with Jesus and are aware of him.

The problem isn't that the Lord withholds his miraculous power. The problem lies with our awareness of it, or rather our unawareness of it. To sharpen our awareness, we can start by listening when others see the Lord's life and Spirit operating in us. Celebrate what they observe! We can reflect on day-to-day "coincidences" that bring his kingdom into sharp focus for us or others. We notice how an answer from our tongue leaps out to help someone, seemingly bypassing our brain. Medical reports come back far less threatening than we'd feared. Time bends in our packed schedule, allowing everything to get done in an atmosphere of ease.

Countless examples of miraculous happenings occur. We just need to be noticing them.

A personal example: the scoliosis curve in my back measured around seventy degrees (anything over forty-five degrees is considered severe), and my right rib was beginning to touch my hip bone. *Painful* is an understatement. I had a vision from the Lord of a stretch exercise, so I did it. Wow—the pain got worse for a day or two. But starting at day three and ever since, there's no pain, and my back curve, although still somewhat obvious, isn't causing any trouble. *Mahanaim!*

Mahanaim dancing—it's our birthright. Join the dance by noticing and **celebrating what you see.**

Intimate Love Mixes with Supernaturalism

Watching the Shulamite twirl the angel dance recharges the king as he once again launches into a description of her beauty (Song of Solomon 7:1–9). He describes in detail parts of her anatomy—with erotic detail in the original language—which we take to understand as his delight in the deepening intimacy they share. This litany of praise and sensual enjoyment leads her to exclaim, "I belong to my lover, and he wants me!" (Song of Solomon 7:10 ERV).

She is wanted by Christ, and hungrily. Being desired for our companionship, our thoughts, and our opinions—*wow!* Being strongly preferred by Jesus brings up what kind of feelings in you? What kind of thoughts? Longings?

Selah

Become comfortable and take some deep breaths. Quiet your cognition, centering your awareness on the king. What has he stirred within you in this chapter?

Focus awareness on the kingdom realm of God that surrounds you now.

When you're ready, ask the Spirit to direct your thoughts to who your "others" are—who in particular he might want you to reach out to, to share gardens with.

What specifics might an encounter with this person/people include, considering your personal angelic escort and the spiritual help the Lord will provide?

_____

_____

Continue to breathe deeply of the supernatural realm that surrounds and fills you. There is a very thin veil at this point between our natural world and Jesus's kingdom.

Ask the Spirit to show you a few specific examples of his supernatural power operating in you right now.

_____

_____

Talk to him about this. What do you long for supernaturally?

_____

_____

Using Immanuel Journaling, ask the Lord to write you a letter, telling you where he wants to go with you supernaturally. This can be in ministry, in relationships, or in your own life. Allow him to take this where he wants to.

Jesus is saying to you, "My favored one, this is what I want for you and me . . ."

_____

_____

Listen to the heart-pounding song #22 in the "*Savor, the Book*" playlist to close your time.

23

REFLECT AND REVIEW

Starting about halfway through chapter 8 in Song of Solomon, we find this puzzling passage:

Song of Solomon 8:8-9 (VOICE):

> (Young Women of Jerusalem): We have a little sister whose breasts have not yet developed. How shall we protect her until the time when she is spoken for? If she is a wall, we will build silver towers of protection; If she is a door, we will barricade the door with the strongest cedar.

This seems to be a throwback to the Shulamite's prior life when she was immature, in bondage and struggling under her old nature. The wording here brings a softness from those early memories of darkness in that the "walls" and "doors" she hid behind were actually protections for her young self. Indeed, many of the strategies we've employed in life were simply early self-protection—needed barriers to protect from further hurt.

But that was then, and this is now.

It can be valuable at this point in the journey to do some review. I'd invite you to grab a beverage of your choice, settle into a comfortable place, and do some reflecting on your life.

Selah

Begin your time submitting your mind and heart to the Lord. Allow deep breathing to usher in his presence. Become aware of his fragrance surrounding you.

Read his words from The Passion Translation—

Song of Solomon 8:5 (TPT):

> When I awakened you under the apple tree, as you were feasting upon me, I awakened your innermost being with the travail of birth as you longed for more of me.

Realize that *he* has awakened you. Reflect upon this feast you've been enjoying from him.

How has this journey been a feast?

_____

Spend a little time simply thanking him for all he's done. Be aware of his reaction as he listens to your words, both verbal and silent.

The above verse also presents the travail of birth. Birth processes are painful and messy. Think about the new birth process throughout this book's journey. What has been the most painful and difficult part?

_____

_____

What has been the most delightful part, or realization?

_____

_____

Allow memories from his words, recorded in this journal or given to you in other contexts of your life, to surface. Be aware of him sitting with you; it's as if you and he are viewing a video of your past months on this journey of intimacy. What do you see in this video? Record the specific highlights and the important revelations you want to refer to in future months:

_____

_____

_____

_____

Write to the Lord (or speak to him sitting there) about how he has changed in your understanding of him . . . what you used to think about him and what you understand now.

_____

_____

_____

_____

What has been the funniest or most endearing quality he's shown you about himself? About yourself?

_____

_____

_____

_____

Now ask him to tell his favorite memory of this journey you've taken together. Wait on this if need be.

_____

_____

When you're ready, reflect with Jesus on what you used to need that now, clothed in his love and experiencing his power within you, you don't need anymore.

I no longer need . . .

_____

_____

Has anything else that used to be a struggle dropped from the burdens you carry?

_____

_____

✳✳✳✳

The Shulamite goes on in 8:9–10 (TPT):

> Now I have grown and become [married], and my love for him has made me a tower of passion and contentment for my beloved. I am now a firm wall of protection for others, guarding them from harm. This is how he sees me—I am the one who brings him bliss, finding favor in his eyes.

Reflect on how *you've* become a tower for Jesus. Is your tower one of peace for him? Or some other atmosphere? Talk to him about the kind of tower you want to provide for him to reside in.

First Corinthians 13:11 says, "When I matured . . . I set aside my childish ways" (TPT). This verse indicates a process of leaving behind childish things (ways of thinking or ways of speaking) that aren't worthy of him or aren't helpful as we mature. Has the love of Christ caused such immature things to fall off you? If so, what are they? (Some examples of childish beliefs: "He doesn't speak to me." "I don't have time to meet with him." "I'm not worthy of his love.")

_____

_____

_____

Finally, you have found his favor. What does this mean to you, practically? In what ways do you see his favor in operation in your life, and how do you want to see more of it?

_____

_____

_____

Celebrate all that this journey has done in your life by listening to song #23 in the "*Savor, the Book*" playlist; sing it as your own.

24

INVITATIONS GOING FORWARD

ONG OF SOLOMON ENDS WITH IMAGERY THAT BECKONS US ONWARD IN OUR JOURNEY OF INTIMACY. We see a picture of the king and the Shulamite enjoying themselves, going to high mountains and discussing the love that now binds them, which is stronger than death. We see a budding partnership between them. No longer is she simply asking for orders; she's initiating in ways she's moved to do. This pictures a fulfillment of Hosea 2:16 (NLT): "[You now] call me 'my husband' instead of 'my master.'" There's a beautiful freedom in their intimate lives—everything shared, everything enjoyed. Then we see the invitations.

1. Invitation to Abundance and Peace

The first invitation toward the onward journey comes from Song of Solomon 8:11: "Solomon had a vineyard at *Baal-hamon*" (emphasis added).

This phrase *Baal-hamon* occurs in Scripture only here. It means "Possessor (or Lord) of abundance." *Solomon* comes from the Hebrew word *shalom*, meaning "peace." The picture is of a person of peace who owns a vast vineyard within which is abundance of every type.

Consider what is included in this little word *shalom*, according to Strong's concordance[28]:

Wholeness	Tranquility
Completeness	Prosperity
Health	Perfectness
Peace	Fullness
Welfare	Rest
Safety	Harmony
Soundness	The absence of agitation or discord

This list sounds abundant to me! All these blessings are ours as we dwell in the Shalom of our Prince of Peace. He invites us to savor often the experiences of being in his vineyard of abundance, this garden of delight, rest, and profusion that he owns. He's provided it; he paid for our free admission to enter, and he loves hanging out with us there.

I was recently watching the shifting colors of a sunset with him. He said, "These colors that you love point to me. The feelings the sunset invokes in you—those are the feelings of intimacy with me. 'The skies proclaim my handiwork.' There's no barrier to your coming, tasting, drinking, and seeing me any time in our private garden. Come in, Val! I want to taste you as much as you want to taste me!"

Jesus says in Song of Solomon 4:9 and 6:5, "With one glance of your eyes, I am undone." On the continuing journey of intimacy, realize that every glance at him during our day, every whispered "I love you, Yeshua," every inside decision to trust and lean on him sends him into joy and ushers our heart into peace and abundance. Give him a side-eye and realize he's watching you with a slow wink. This mutual love, enjoyment, and strong commitment is the completion of what he died for: His love given on the cross, being reciprocated by the objects of his love. Completion: the consummation of the Trinity's plan since the garden of Eden. Our private garden is the key to all this.

2. Invitation to Mountain Living

The mountain theme in Song of Solomon begins in chapter 2 with the king bounding and leaping over mountains and continues through the last verse in chapter 8. Mountains are our king's habitat. They imply spiritual high places that we're invited to (see Colossians 3:1–3). He wants us with him in his high kingdom atmosphere, which implies our dwelling *above* the stuff of the world: above the anxieties of materialism and information overload. As we lean back into the love of Jesus and learn to dwell with him in intimacy, taming our mind and entering into all the gospel has given us, we revel in the ordinary places of life that now seem tinged with shimmering possibility. These high mountains are where the king invited the Shulamite in chapter 4, and his invitation is open to us today.

My husband and I live in Woodland Park, Colorado, known as "the city above the clouds." An interesting inversion factor in the weather here has us basking in the sun at 8,500 feet while a blanket of clouds shrouds Colorado Springs, 2,000 feet below us. It's a beautiful reminder of where Jesus invites his bride to live— up above the mist, confusion, and murkiness of life in this world. The sun and beautiful sky await as we accept his invitation!

3. Invitation to Love That's a Fire

The love of Christ is a fierce, unyielding force we don't want to play around with or mock as we continue the journey.

Song of Solomon 8:6–7 (TPT):

> (Jesus): Fasten me upon your heart as a **seal** of fire forevermore. This living, consuming flame will seal you as my prisoner of love. My passion is stronger than the chains of death and the grave, all-consuming as the very flashes of fire from the burning heart of God. Place this fierce, unrelenting fire over your entire being. Rivers of pain and persecution will never extinguish this flame. Endless floods will be unable to quench this raging fire that burns within you. (emphasis added)

The love of God is far beyond our human understanding of what we generally refer to as "love."

- It's a boiling river coming straight from God's heart—white-hot and pure.

- It's an unending fire: warmth and provision.

- It's unquenchable: not snuffed out by persecution, hardship, pain, or adversity. These things merely stoke the flame and render our lives even more passionately his.

Safe within the strong cords of Jesus's passionate love, we step out of fear and into the boxing ring of our culture. With newfound supernatural help, we find fresh courage to stand up and fight for those struggling and to speak out when the name and character of our king are being defamed. Concern for what others think gets bulldozed under the bubbling laughter of his presence and personality. Persecution, threats, prison . . . what are those to us whose future is assured?

And *oh!* The sublime pleasures he has in store for his lovers! The English language simply cannot describe the fullness of his love as we experience it in full-brain mode. If he seems too good to be true, it's probably Jesus!

4. Invitation to Take Our Full Place in His Family

This love described is like a wedding ring in significance. The word *seal* in the passage above is *signet* in Hebrew, or the ring that, dipped in wax, substituted for the signature of the bearer. It denotes belonging to the family whose crest was on the signet. Wearing this ring and using it in the marketplace implied commitment and honor from each party—the giver and the receiver.

There is an invitation to responsibility for us here. As we figuratively accept this signet, we're agreeing to live lives worthy of him, to represent him—his love and truth—as accurately as we are able. We accept the missions he invites us into. We turn from childish complaining or whining. In a word, we live more for him and his kingdom than for our own small world.

Selah

Final deep breaths. Stop and *savor* being loved in this strong, unrelenting passion of the king of the universe. Speak to yourself the adjectives you feel in your body now and in your emotions or soul.

Within the vineyard of relationship with him are provision, abundance, peace, and the meeting of every longing we have. Consider what you'd like in your life for it to be more abundant. What do you need to be free of in order to dwell in an abundant vineyard?

_____

_____

Review the descriptors contained in *shalom* above. Do any stand out?

_____

_____

With your palms open and turned up on your lap, ask the Lord to give you the abundance he wants to give you going forward. This may come as a picture in your mind, a scripture, words written in your mind's eye, or a sense.

Are there mountains in your life that he's ready to scale with you? How can you move out into freedom—to do what he puts on your heart, to be the person he says you are—and hike the heights?

_____

_____

Now look at the image[29] of the signet ring above. Such a ring was given to those who had been trusted to speak on behalf of the father of the family, to use the family's authority to do business in its name.

Imagine the father giving you such a ring and asking you to accept the responsibility, benefits, and incredible privilege of wearing that ring.

As you reflect on this with the Lord, what does accepting this signet ring mean to you?

_____

Is there anything you'd like to express to him of your fear, commitment, or willingness to receive this ring?

_____

_____

Ask the Lord what specifically he'd like you to realize as you accept this *signet* ring of his family.

_____

_____

Write in your own words your desire for his love's fire, your commitment to him, and/or any trepidation as you move further in this journey of intimacy. Be as honest as possible:

_____

_____

_____

Allow him to write you back:

_____

_____

Listen to song #24 in the "*Savor, the Book*" playlist, reveling in worship as you accept these invitations of the king going forward.

As this short journey in Song of Solomon comes to an end, realize that we've only dipped our toe into the edges of sublime oneness with King Jesus. The journey continues throughout eternity. . . .

(And we thought we knew what love was!)

ACKNOWLEDGMENTS

No book is ever written by one person alone. Savor has had many voices speaking into it and I'm grateful to each of you.

Megan, you are the world's best editor, who has become a dear friend. Your enthusiastic support for and editing genius of this book have made all the difference. Thank you.

Rachel, Shannon, Jonathan, Aria, and Bethany, you are the real deal in Christian editing and publishing. Expertise off the charts plus your warm support and help have been invaluable. How do you answer emails so quickly?

Laura, Melanie, Tiffany and Teresa, steering committee for the "Kiss of God" retreat that birthed these pages, you each have shaped the message of *Savor* and have deeply enriched my life in the process. Thank you for your friendship and for sharing your gifts.

To all the women who attended the Kiss of God retreat—you know who you are!—thank you for being willing to test-drive this material and for cheering on the message of *Savor.*

Chris and Tiff, leaders and friends at Emmaus Fellowship in Woodland Park . . . What can I say but a huge thank-you for friendship, teaching, leadership, and tons of fun with backpacks on our backs? You have helped shape my life for decades; your influence is all over these pages.

To all the Navigator friends and coworkers across the globe whom Bob and I have been privileged to share life with—thank you for your friendship, kindness, and dedication to serving the King of Kings.

Finally, to my husband, Bob: Thanks for putting up with countless faraway stares from me as my mind was in book-land and I wasn't listening very well. I love you.

APPENDIX

Savor, the Book playlist:

Chapter 1 – "Be Still and Know" - Jeremy Riddle

Chapter 2 – "Kinda Wild" - JUDAH

Chapter 3 – "My Soul Rests" - One Hope Project

Chapter 4 – "Simple" - Melanie Tierce

Chapter 5 – "I See Grace" - Micah Tyler

Chapter 6 – "Holy Eyes" - 7 Hills Worship

Chapter 7 – "Repentance Reimagined" - Gable Price

Chapter 8 – "Miracle of the Mind" - Amanda Cook

Chapter 9 – "I Am Your Beloved", Bethel Music, Jonathan David Helser

Chapter 10 – "I Am" - JUDAH

Chapter 11 – "The Getting Through" - JUDAH and Amanda Cook

Chapter 12 – "Oceans" (Stripped Acoustic) - Andreas Moe

Chapter 13 – "Kind" - Ben Potter

Chapter 14 – "Communion" - Maverick City Music with Steffany

Chapter 15 – "Good and Loved" - Travis Greene with Steffany

Chapter 16 – "Lost in Your Love" - Brandon Lake and Sarah Reeves

Chapter 17 – "Closer" - Maverick City Music (featuring Brandon Lake)

Chapter 18 – "New Wine" - Hillsong Worship and Brooke Ligertwood

Chapter 19 – "Girl" - SYML

Chapter 20 – "Hineni" - Sarah Lieberman

Chapter 21 – "DNA" - Apollo LTD

Chapter 22 – "Count 'Em" - Brandon Lake

Chapter 23 – "We Are Brave" - Shawn McDonald

Chapter 24 – "Endless Alleluia" - Cory Asbury

NOTES

Epigraph

1. *Cambridge Dictionary*, s.v. "savor," accessed December 16, 2023, https://dictionary.cambridge.org/dictionary/english/savor.

2. *The Free Dictionary*, s.v. "savor," accessed December 16, 2023, https://www.thefreedictionary.com/Savor.

Introduction

3. Dictionary.com, s.v. "intimacy," accessed December 16, 2023, https://www.dictionary.com/browse/intimacy.

4. Gloria Wilcox, *The Feeling Wheel* (Greater New York Hospital Association, 1982).

5. Wikipedia, s.v. "Lectio Divina," last modified October 22, 2023, https://en.wikipedia.org/wiki/Lectio_Divina.

6. Wikipedia, "Lectio Divina."

7. Jim Wilder, "Immanuel Journaling," Presence and Practice, 2014, https://www.presenceandpractice.com/immanuel-journaling.

8. "Neuroplasticity," *Psychology Today*, accessed December 16, 2023, https://www.psychologytoday.com/us/basics/neuroplasticity.

9. Image of two chairs on beach and image of backpack created by author using Canva.

Chapter 1

10. Israel Knohl, "YHWH: The Original Arabic Meaning of the Name," thetorah.com, accessed December 16, 2023, https://www.thetorah.com/article/yhwh-the-original-arabic-meaning-of-the-name.

11. *Vocabulary.com* dictionary, s.v. "impassioned," accessed December 16, 2023, https://www.vocabulary.com/dictionary/impassioned.

Chapter 2

12. John Burke, essay in *Imagine Heaven: Near-Death Experiences, God's Promises, and the Exhilarating Future That Awaits You* (Grand Rapids, MI: Baker Books, 2020), 156.

13. Burke, essay in Imagine Heaven, 172.

Chapter 6

14. Image of lion used under license from Shutterstock.com.

Chapter 10

15. "Centering Prayer," Contemplative Outreach, Ltd., accessed April 11, 2023, https://www.contemplativeoutreach.org/centering-prayer-method/.

Chapter 11

16. Image of fox used under license from Shutterstock.com.

Chapter 12

17. Wikipedia, s.v. "Dark Night of the Soul," last modified November 6, 2023, https://en.wikipedia.org/wiki/Dark_Night_of_the_Soul.

Chapter 13

18. Image of Jesus by water created by author using Canva.

Chapter 14

19. Burke, essay in *Imagine Heaven*, 190.

20. Burke, 190.

Chapter 15

21. Charles Spurgeon, "Christ's Estimate of His People," The Spurgeon Center, January 23, 1859, https://www.spurgeon.org/resource-library/sermons/christs -estimate-of-his-people/#flipbook/.

Chapter 16

22. Image of tunnel created by author using Canva.

Chapter 17

23. Mary Mrozowski, "The Welcoming Prayer," milehighmin.org, accessed June 23, 2020, https://milehighmin.org/the-welcoming-prayer-2020/.

Chapter 18

24. Definition of "trust" from Google online dictionary.

25. Image of man on cliff ("trust") used under license from Shutterstock.com.

26. Image of gates created by author using Canva.

Chapter 19

27. Image of veil created by author using Canva.

Chapter 24

28. "Meaning of the Word 'Shalom,'" The Refiner's Fire, accessed December 16, 2023, https://www.therefinersfire.org/meaning_of_shalom.htm.

29. Image of signet ring used under license from Shutterstock.com.